Rail freight since 1968
BULK FREIGHT

Rail freight since 1968

BULK FREIGHT

Paul Shannon

· RAILWAY HERITAGE ·
from
The NOSTALGIA Collection

First published in 2008

British Library Cataloguing in Publication Data

A catalogue record for this book is available from the British Library.

ISBN 978 1 85794 299 6

Silver Link Publishing Ltd
The Trundle
Ringstead Road
Great Addington
Kettering
Northants NN14 4BW

Tel/Fax: 01536 330588
email: sales@nostalgiacollection.com
Website: www.nostalgiacollection.com

Printed and bound in the Czech Republic

All photographs are by the author unless otherwise credited.

Half title Nos 37160 and 37127 pass Abington with 6S83, the 1205 Clitheroe to Gunnie cement train, on 15 July 1988. This flow ceased in 1993, but resumed in 2008 to a new terminal at Mossend.

Frontispiece With the access siding to Dove Holes Quarry visible on the left, Nos 20172 and 20077 throb past Peak Forest South signal box with 6F43, the 1539 limestone train from Tunstead to Oakleigh, on 1 September 1984.

Below The British Steel exchange sidings at Lackenby are pictured on 24 August 1994, with GEC 0-6-0 diesel-hydraulic No 266 positioning a load of hot rolled coil for a mainline departure while Nos 37426 and 37716 arrive with a slab train from Scunthorpe.

A Silver Link book
from
The NOSTALGIA *Collection*

Contents

Preface

Few would doubt that rail freight's greatest strength is its ability to carry large tonnages of bulk materials directly between its customers' terminals. British industry in the late 1960s provided plenty of opportunities to exploit this strength. Regular flows of raw materials and semi-finished products for the steel industry were already well established, while the tonnages of petroleum products moved by rail increased fourfold from 1962 to 1972 as the oil companies developed networks of rail-fed distribution terminals. And then there was aggregates traffic, with numerous flows starting up from quarries in the Mendips, Leicestershire and Derbyshire.

The expansion of bulk rail freight required investment in suitable terminals and rolling-stock. BR's once nationwide network of public goods depots gradually withered away in favour of privately owned facilities for oil, aggregates, cement, steel or whatever. The use of BR rolling-stock on many bulk flows was phased out as customers introduced their own fleets of wagons. The fact that customers had to provide much of the investment was a strong incentive for them to stay with rail.

During the 1970s rail freight suffered increasing pressure from road haulage, where costs were falling and journey times were shrinking. On the positive side, the Government offered to contribute up to 60% of terminal and rolling-stock costs through Section 8 of the 1974 Transport Act. Many bulk flows benefited from this scheme, with grants totalling some £69 million being awarded over a 20-year period.

In the harsh economic climate of the 1980s, BR was divided into business sectors and Railfreight faced stringent financial targets. In December 1989 the Secretary of State announced that Railfreight should achieve an annual return of 8% on all new investment, that it should make a £50 million profit by 1992-3, and that the bulk arm of the business should achieve an 8% annual return on all its assets by 1994-5. A weeding-out of unprofitable rail freight services became inevitable.

While wagonload bore the brunt of the cutbacks, some trainload services were also vulnerable, especially those with small payloads or which made sole use of expensive freight-only infrastructure. Further losses resulted from changes in industry, such as the closure of Ravenscraig steelworks. The bulk flows with the best prospects were those where train tonnages could be increased to exploit the power of BR's new fleet of Class 60 locomotives or, in the case of Mendip stone, the privately owned Class 59s.

The privatisation of BR in the 1990s brought renewed optimism for rail freight, as the three bulk freight divisions – Transrail, Loadhaul and Mainline Freight – fought to increase their market share, a policy that continued once those divisions were recombined as English Welsh & Scottish Railway. Between 1994 and 2004 the amount of freight moved by rail annually, excluding coal traffic, rose by more than 40%. Not that EWS was always the winner: Blue Circle's decision to contract some of its cement traffic to Freightliner in 2000 was one of the first tangible results of competition in the rail freight market. And EWS's acquisition of 250 General Motors Class 66 locomotives paved the way for its competitors to buy the same locomotive design off the shelf, giving them a quick foothold in the market as contracts came up for renewal. Nevertheless, at the time of writing EWS is still the dominant haulier of bulk rail freight in the UK.

1.

Aggregates

Carryings of sand, gravel and stone by rail increased dramatically in the 1970s, as a huge boom in the construction industry coincided with the realisation that local supplies of these materials in key areas such as South East England were quickly running out. This was the era of frantic motorway construction and of proliferating building projects, some supported by copious government funding and others by a buoyant and ambitious private sector. It was also a time when the gravel pits in the Thames Valley and elsewhere were getting bigger and ever closer to residential areas and, even if more supplies lay underground, it was becoming less environmentally acceptable to extract them.

The shortfall in local supplies of aggregate in the South East was made up by moving large tonnages of crushed rock from the Mendips and Leicestershire. In both cases the distances were great enough to give rail a keen competitive edge over road, all the more so because the stone could easily be moved in trainload quantities, without the complications and costs associated with wagonload shunting and tripping. The tonnage of aggregates carried by BR grew from just 2 million tonnes in 1969 to almost 10 million tonnes by 1974 – a far more dramatic rise than Dr Beeching might have hoped for back in the early 1960s. The growth was largely concentrated on the South East, but there were also significant pockets of activity in North West England and in West Yorkshire.

The rail freight industry and its customers had to find new resources quickly to cater for the growth of the 1970s. Suitable receiving terminals were provided either by adapting existing sidings, such as former station goods yards or coal depots, or by installing new facilities. BR covered the short-term need for rolling-stock by redeploying hopper and tippler wagons that had previously carried coal, iron ore or other minerals. This second-hand stock, all vacuum-braked, was gradually replaced by modern air-braked vehicles that would be owned by or leased to the customer. This was in line with BR's policy of not providing wagons for most traffic flows other than coal and steel. Much of the investment in new receiving terminals and rolling-stock was supported by government grants under Section 8 of the 1974 Transport Act, covering up to 60% of the set-up costs for traffic flows that otherwise might have gone by road.

In the 1980s and 1990s the overall tonnage of aggregates carried by rail fluctuated in line with the fortunes of the construction industry – and therefore the state of the economy. The business grew particularly fast in the late 1980s, reaching a peak of 18 million tonnes before declining sharply to less than 11 million tonnes in 1993. It then recovered, reaching around 20 million tonnes in the early 2000s. Some of the growth came from existing markets, but EWS was also successful in gaining aggregate flows from new sources in South Wales and Dorset.

The monopoly of EWS on aggregate traffic was challenged in late 2002, when newly formed company Freightliner Heavy Haul operated a trial train of slate waste from Blaenau Ffestiniog – a potential long-term flow that is unfortunately still 'on the back burner' at the time of writing. Heavy Haul then won a short-term flow of slag from Port Clarence to Chesterton Junction in 2003,

Above The stone terminal at Angerstein Wharf received trainloads of stone from the Mendips and Leicestershire as well as forwarding sea-dredged aggregates by rail to various local terminals. No 56037 shunts Bardon hoppers at Angerstein Wharf on 9 August 1990 after arriving with 6Z55, the 2320 from Merehead.

Right ICI began moving limestone from Tunstead to its Hindlow lime-making plant in January 1988 after the end of quarrying at Hindlow. Nos 37679 and 37683 have just arrived at Hindlow with 7T81, the 0915 train from Tunstead, on 9 April 1988.

Left Limestone dust momentarily fills the air as No 59101 passes Berkley with 7O48, the 0831 from Whatley to Hamworthy, on 4 April 2007. The hoppers at the front of the train are for Theale and will be detached at Westbury.

followed by several flows of limestone from the Peak District and, crucially, a five-year contract with Aggregate Industries in 2006 to run trains from Leicestershire, South Wales and Dorset. Today Heavy Haul operates its own fleet of flat-bottomed bogie open wagons (MJA) and two types of hopper wagon (HIA and JGA), putting the company in a strong competitive position for potential new flows.

The railway's overall market share of aggregate traffic continues to vary widely between different regions, with a figure of more than 25% for flows from South West England – predominantly limestone from the Mendips – but only 14% for traffic from Yorkshire and Humberside. The minimum economic distance for a rail-borne aggregate flow is generally reckoned to be 30 miles, but shorter-distance flows can succeed where there are planning constraints on road movements, eg in central London, or where there is an exceptionally large volume on a single route.

For the future, experts predict limited opportunities for further growth in rail-borne aggregates. In a market study carried out in 2004, the Strategic Rail Authority concluded that the railway might achieve annual growth of between 1% and 2%. Planning constraints are expected to curb the extraction of primary aggregates, ie aggregates from quarries and pits, and any expansion in rail business is likely to come from secondary aggregates, such as china clay waste. Another limitation on rail traffic might be planning constraints on new receiving terminals close to the point of consumption; several potential sites have already been rejected for this reason.

South West and South Wales

Aggregate traffic in South West England is dominated by two limestone quarries in the Mendip Hills of Somerset – Merehead and Whatley. From modest beginnings more than 30 years ago, rail-borne traffic from Merehead and Whatley has grown to reach an annual total of around 6 million tonnes at the time of writing.

The loading facilities at Merehead date back to 1970, when Foster Yeoman expanded its quarrying operation at Torr Works, Merehead, to supplement its long-established quarry at Dulcote, near Wells. Foster Yeoman had previously relied on local outlets for modest quantities of stone. The company installed automated loading facilities at Merehead in the form of an overhead 'tripper', which received stone from the crusher via a conveyor system and could load a complete rake of wagons on either of two parallel sidings without the need for a shunting locomotive. The rail access to the quarry was improved in 1973 by the building of a new south-to-north spur, resulting in the triangular layout that exists today.

Initially the trains from Merehead consisted of second-hand railway-owned wagons – mainly MSV iron ore tipplers and HTV coal hoppers – but in 1972 Foster Yeoman began using the first of a sizeable fleet of air-braked PGA two-axle hopper wagons, leased from Procor. The 1980s marked a shift from two-axle to bogie wagons: first Foster Yeoman took on a fleet of former bogie iron ore tipplers (PTA, later recoded JTA/JUA) that had been made redundant by the closure of Consett steelworks, and in 1984 the company ordered a fleet of 37 purpose-built aluminium-bodied bogie hoppers (PHA). Unfortunately the PHAs suffered from structural defects and all were withdrawn by 1989. However, the late 1980s saw the introduction of two further wagon types built by Orenstein & Koppel, which are still in use at the time of writing: 61 PHA (later JYA) bogie open box wagons and 100 PHA (later JHA) bogie hopper wagons.

The loading sidings at Merehead were lengthened in 1983 to enable trains with a payload of more than 2,500 tonnes to be handled. In 1986 a 'shuttle' loader was installed on the third loading siding, capable of loading a 100-tonne wagon in less than 2 minutes – albeit requiring the use of a locomotive to position each wagon in turn under the loader. By this time Foster Yeoman had built its own locomotive and rolling-stock maintenance facilities at Merehead, located within the triangle of lines just outside the loading terminal.

By the mid-1980s BR was moving more than 3 million tonnes of limestone from Merehead each year, which was around 75% of the quarry's output. Regular trains operated to around 15 receiving depots, mostly in and around London but

Before the massive expansion of quarrying at Merehead and Whatley, 'Hymek' No D7007 passes Frome town centre on the Radstock branch with a stone train from Hapsford on 29 December 1967. *Hugh Ballantyne*

Class 52 'Western' No D1072 *Western Glory* takes the Westbury station line at Fairwood Junction on 19 August 1972 with empty 'House Coal Concentration' hoppers that have been redeployed on Mendip stone traffic. *Hugh Ballantyne*

EMD switcher No 44 draws its rake of JHA hopper wagons forward on siding No 3 at Merehead on 3 April 2007. On the left are sidings 1 and 2, topped by the conveyor belt that feeds the 'tripper'.

including Eastleigh and Botley in Hampshire and Wootton Bassett near Swindon. The huge terminal in Theale was built with the support of a £1.8 million Section 8 Grant. Another significant step forward was the opening of Foster Yeoman's Purfleet terminal in 1984, enabling the closure of three smaller railheads at Angerstein Wharf, Pitsea and Chadwell Heath. Alongside the core network, several temporary railheads were established for construction projects, such as Taplow and Newbury for the M4 motorway, Longcross and Winchfield for the M3 motorway, and Tonbridge for the M25/M26 motorways.

A brief period of haulage by Class 56 locomotives from May 1983 was followed by Foster Yeoman's ground-breaking decision to provide its own motive power, the General Motors Class 59. From May 1986 a single Class 59 was diagrammed to haul trains with a gross laden weight of 4,300 tonnes, which had previously required a pair of Class 56s. The practice of running multi-portion trains between Merehead and Acton was soon established, splitting into two

or three feeder services to individual terminals such as Purfleet, Crawley and Harlow Mill.

Foster Yeoman was keen to maximise efficiency by running ever longer trains, and to that end a remarkable trial took place on the night of 25/26 May 1991, with two Class 59s hauling a trailing load of just under 12,000 tonnes. Although the trial had to be cut short because of damage caused by weaknesses in the wagon couplings, the two General Motors locomotives moved the train successfully and their remarkable haulage capability was proven.

●

Whatley Quarry dates back to 1937 when it was owned by Roads Reconstruction and known as New Frome Quarry. It was taken over by the Amey Roadstone Corporation (ARC) in the late 1960s and the former narrow-gauge mineral line serving the quarry was reconstructed as a standard gauge railway suitable for use by BR traction. Today Whatley is owned by the multi-national firm Hanson; it has an annual output of up to 5

					Foster Yeoman sample programme, November 1987
Code	Dep	Days	From	To	
6E52	0034	EWD	Merehead	Purfleet	also traffic for Crawley EWD and Harlow Mill SX
6A29	0300	SX	Merehead	Theale	
6A24	0343	SO	Merehead	Acton	
7Z62	0425	SX	Merehead	Harlow Mill	also traffic for Crawley WFO and Purfleet TThO
6Z42	0540	MSX	Merehead	Wootton Bassett	
6A42	0717	MO	Merehead	Wootton Bassett	
6O44	0718	MSX	Merehead	Eastleigh	
6Z88	0745	SO	Merehead	Woking	
7Z88	0840	MWFO	Merehead	Woking	
8C63	1147	ThO	Merehead	Taunton	
6Z30	1320	TO	Merehead	Wootton Bassett	
6A30	1420	MWFO	Merehead	Theale	
6Z30	1420	ThO	Merehead	Eastleigh	
6Z48	1540	MSX	Merehead	Acton	
6A20	1634	SX	Merehead	Brentford	
6O75	1718	SX	Merehead	Eastleigh	
6O47	2031	FSX	Merehead	Botley	
6Z50	2031	FO	Merehead	Brentford	

Harlow Mill was one of a number of former station goods yards that became dedicated to aggregates traffic. No 59005 propels a mixture of PXA, PTA and PHA wagons into the discharge siding at Harlow Mill on 14 July 1989, having worked a feeder service from Acton. The terminal was later expanded to handle Bardon as well as Foster Yeoman traffic.

No 56031 *Merehead* departs from Whatley with 7O83, the 1209 train to Fareham, on 19 February 1988.

The unique Ruston Paxman-engined Class 47/9 No 47901 worked out of Westbury alongside a pool of Class 56 locomotives. It is pictured passing Botley on 18 August 1987 with the 1120 stone train from Whatley to Fareham.

million tonnes of which roughly 50% moves by rail.

Rail traffic from Whatley grew rapidly in the 1970s, with trains serving a network of terminals similar to those supplied from Merehead. After a spell of relying on elderly BR wagons, ARC acquired its first batch of 64 two-axle PGA hopper wagons in 1972; the company then leased further batches of PGAs from Procor with the last examples entering service in 1981. ARC also leased two batches of air-braked bogie open box wagons: one batch comprised former iron ore tipplers, coded PTA, and the other was a small fleet of purpose-built vehicles of similar design to the tipplers but coded PXA.

ARC opened major new rail handling facilities at Whatley in October 1987, costing £8.5 million and supported by a £3.7 million Section 8 Grant. The timetable for January 1988 shows an average of nine daily departures from Whatley, serving railheads at Theale, Oxford, Appleford, West Drayton, Hayes & Harlington, Ripple Lane, Woking, Tolworth, Chislehurst, Allington, Hothfield, Bat & Ball, Ardingly, Fareham and Totton. The Hayes & Harlington train operated on behalf of Tarmac, who shared ARC's loading facilities at Whatley at that time.

The use of BR Class 56s out of Whatley was phased out as ARC introduced its four Class 59 locomotives from October 1990. The Class 59s enabled a significant increase in train lengths, with two daily trains to the London area now conveying two portions each and with the Theale train almost doubled in size. During 1990 ARC also took delivery of 145 new JHA bogie hopper wagons with low-track-force bogies, built by Powell Duffryn and Procor.

While the Mendip business in the 1970s and 1980s was dominated by Foster Yeoman and ARC, BR also carried limestone from a loading point at

ARC sample programme, November 1987

Code	Dep	Days	From	To	
7E66	0013	MSX	Whatley	Ripple Lane	also traffic to Chislehurst
7E66	0050	MO	Whatley	Ripple Lane	also traffic to Chislehurst
6O38	0110	TThO	Whatley	Tolworth	
7A15	0135	SX	Whatley	Appleford	
6O55	0235	SO	Whatley	Salfords	
6O80	0636	MWO	Whatley	Allington	
6A17	0745	SX	Whatley	Theale	
6O53	0803	WFO	Whatley	Totton	
6Z62	0803	MO	Whatley	West Drayton	
6Z82	0803	TThO	Whatley	Southall	traffic for Hothfield
7O83	1209	ThSX	Whatley	Fareham	
6O40	1909	FSX	Whatley	Ardingly	
6A03	1950	SX	Whatley	West Drayton	
6O95	2107	TO	Whatley	Hothfield	
6O95	2107	MWO	Whatley	Bat & Ball	
6M20	0220	SX	Stoke Gifford*	Wolverton	*traffic from Tytherington
6O80	0510	FO	Stoke Gifford**	Allington	**traffic from Machen
6M24	0645	SX	Tytherington	Wolverton	
6O95	2125	MO	Stoke Gifford*	Bat & Ball	*traffic from Tytherington
6O96	2124	ThO	Stoke Gifford*	Hothfield	*traffic from Tytherington
6O96	2200	SuO	Stoke Gifford*	Hothfield	*traffic from Tytherington
6O87	2355	SuO	Stoke Gifford*	Allington	*traffic from Tytherington
6O87	2355	SX	Stoke Gifford*	Allington	*traffic from Tytherington

Carrying the short-lived 'large logo' Railfreight livery, No 56056 passes under the loader at Tytherington Quarry with 6C72, the 1410 empties from Stoke Gifford, on 27 July 1987. After loading, the train would depart as 6C23 to Stoke Gifford, feeding into 6M20 to Wolverton.

Frome, destined for the Bardon receiving terminal at Thorney Mill. However, this flow was switched to run from Merehead in 1988.

Rail access to a second ARC quarry at Tytherington, north of Bristol, was provided in 1972 by re-opening a 6-mile stretch of the former Thornbury branch, originally closed in 1967. Using the sidings at Stoke Gifford as a staging point, BR ran block trains from Tytherington to various discharge terminals in South East England; those in use in the late 1980s included Wolverton, Allington, Hothfield and Bat & Ball. Regular flows from Tytherington declined in the 1990s, but the branch continued to see periods of use for both outward traffic and inward movements of Mendip limestone for blending.

●

The formation of Mendip Rail in 1993 brought the resources of Foster Yeoman (later Aggregate Industries) and ARC (later Hanson) under a common management. From now the locomotives and wagons belonging to the two companies could be used on each other's services where it made good practical sense to do so.

One of the first successes for Mendip Rail was a contract to move more than 1.5 million tonnes of limestone from Merehead and Whatley to Henbury, near Avonmouth, for the building of the second River Severn motorway crossing. Further short-term contracts in the 1990s included more than 300,000 tonnes of stone to Avonmouth for a

Honda car plant, 500,000 tonnes of stone to Exeter and Hamworthy for A30 an A35 upgrade projects, 20,000 tonnes of stone to Torbay for Eurobell telephone cable works, and 100,000 tonnes of sea defence stone to Minehead.

The Minehead traffic was the first revenue-earning freight on the West Somerset Railway since BR withdrew goods services on the branch in 1964. A total of 239 loaded trains ran between March 1997 and June 1998, mostly hauled by a single Class 37 locomotive and each conveying between 500 and 1,050 tonnes of stone. The contract brought a short-term reprieve for 25 vacuum-braked YCV 'Turbot' wagons whose short length and light axle loadings made them suited to the task.

During 1999 Mendip Rail moved 85,000 tonnes of stone from Merehead and Whatley to Thames Haven for a new gas-fired power station. An even bigger prize was the contract to move some 1.6 million tonnes of stone from Merehead to Sevington for the Lenham to Dollands Moor section of the Channel Tunnel Rail Link, plus 250,000 tonnes from Whatley to Allington for the North Downs Tunnel. Two further short-term flows operated to the West Somerset Railway, one in 2000 for sea defence work and the second in 2004 for road repairs. With the 'Turbots' now withdrawn, these two flows used air-braked wagons hauled by Class 59 or Class 66 traction.

Regular and short-term flows from the Mendips benefited from the introduction of 90 JNA bogie

No 59205 passes Wanstrow on the Merehead branch with 7C77, the 1240 empties from Acton to Merehead, on 4 April 2007. The train includes JNA wagons from Harlow and Woking and KEA wagons from Battersea.

box wagons in 2000-01. Built by Marcroft and leased to Mendip Rail by Nacco, this was the first rolling-stock fleet to carry Mendip Rail rather than Foster Yeoman or ARC/Hanson branding. Also drafted into the Mendip Rail wagon fleet were more than 90 KEA/JNA bogie box wagons that had previously carried either ballast or Channel Tunnel concrete segments. Other wagon types have appeared from time to time to cover shortages, such as Tiphook-owned KPA hoppers and, in 2006, former National Power JHA hoppers.

At the time of writing the busiest single destination terminal for Mendip stone is Theale, which received more than 400,000 tonnes in 2006. Theale handles stone of numerous different grades, as do other Aggregate Industries-operated depots such as Acton, Botley, Crawley and Purfleet. In a similar way Hanson handles a range of grades at its own receiving depots such as Allington, Ardingly, Dagenham, Fareham and West Drayton. The smaller Hanson quarry at Tytherington continues to see limited use, mainly incoming traffic from Whatley for local distribution. Both Merehead and Whatley also serve general distribution terminals owned by third parties, such as Brentford (Day Group), Crawley (Cemex) and – a recent addition to the programme – the Tarmac terminal at St Pancras.

While some of the destination terminals have been regular fixtures in the train plan for more than 30 years, others have either come and gone or may operate intermittently on a 'campaign' basis. Chichester is a relatively new destination for Mendip stone, while Oxford Banbury Road was reinstated in 2006 after many years of disuse. A temporary terminal was set up at Colnbrook for the construction of Terminal 5 at Heathrow Airport. The depots at Exeter, Sevington and East Peckham all operate on a 'campaign' basis, receiving a batch of 10 to 15 trains over a two-to-three-week period to build stocks that last for several months.

The weekly train plan comprises a mixture of single-portion and multi-portion or 'jumbo' trains. The single-portion trains tend to serve destinations that are relatively close to the quarries, such as Theale, Wootton Bassett and Eastleigh. The heaviest single-portion train runs from Merehead to Theale with between 36 and 42 bogie wagons. The 'jumbo' trains each convey traffic for up to three different destinations in London and the South East, splitting into feeder services at Acton yard. The maximum loading on these services is an impressive 44 bogie wagons,

and even then the limiting factor is not the haulage capability of the locomotive but infrastructure constraints such as the length of Woodborough loop. Trains conveying Orenstein & Koppel wagons can be difficult to path because these wagons have poor riding characteristics and are subject to a 45mph speed restriction.

Both Merehead and Whatley quarries appear to have good medium-term prospects. Aggregate

Foster Yeoman sample programme, March 2007

Code	Dep	Days	From	To	
7A29	0215	EWD	Merehead	Theale	
7A09	0712	MTThO	Merehead	Acton	traffic for Acton (Forticrete), Purfleet and Brentford
7A09	0712	WFO	Merehead	Acton	traffic for Acton (Forticrete), Purfleet and Crawley
7A17	1033	SX	Merehead	Acton	traffic for Acton and Colnbrook
7B14	1038	TO	Merehead	Wootton Bassett	
7O40	1340	SX	Merehead	Eastleigh	
7A15	1708	SX	Merehead	Acton	traffic for Crawley and Colnbrook
7C59	2025	SX	Merehead	Westbury	traffic for Botley
6A91	2240	SuWO	Merehead	Acton	traffic for Purley, Battersea and Woking
6A91	2240	MO	Merehead	Acton	traffic for Purley, Woking and Purfleet
6A91	2240	TThO	Merehead	Acton	traffic for Harlow Mill, Battersea and Woking

Hanson sample programme, March 2007

Code	Dep	Days	From	To	
7A71	0028	TSO	Whatley	Acton	traffic for West Drayton
7O52	0253	TSX	Whatley	Chichester	
7B13	0440	TWFO	Whatley	Wootton Bassett	
6C14	0510	MTThO	Whatley	Westbury	traffic for Oxford Banbury Road
6C14	0510	WFO	Whatley	Westbury	traffic for Appleford
7O48	0922	TWThO	Whatley	Hamworthy	
6A74	0922	MO	Whatley	Theale	
6Z20	0945	SX	Whatley	St Pancras	
7A31	1324	WSX	Whatley	Acton	traffic for Dagenham and West Drayton
7A31	1324	WO	Whatley	Acton	traffic for Dagenham and Hayes
7C57	2023	SuO+FSX	Whatley	Westbury	traffic for Fareham and Exeter
6A20	2048	SuTThO	Whatley	Acton	traffic for Allington and Ardingly
6A20	2048	MO	Whatley	Acton	traffic for Allington and Radlett
6A20	2048	WO	Whatley	Acton	traffic for Allington and Hothfield

Industries has been granted planning permission to quarry an additional 95 million tonnes of stone at Merehead, extending its life until 2030. Likewise Whatley has planning consent for at least another 20 years.

●

Two terminals in the Bristol area have acted as loading points for aggregates in recent years. One was Bristol East Depot, where stone from the Tarmac quarry at Flax Bourton was dispatched by rail to Hayes & Harlington in 1999. The other was the port of Avonmouth, where gritstone from Ireland was dispatched to Crawley and Theale from 2006 onwards.

In Devon a long-standing source of railway ballast is Meldon Quarry, which once operated as a wholly owned subsidiary of BR and produced up to 1 million tonnes of metamorphosed sandstone a year for the Southern and Western Regions. In the early 1980s Meldon had four scheduled departures each weekday – one to Taunton, one to Bristol and two to Salisbury. In 1994 the quarry and the 20-mile branch line from Crediton were sold to CAMAS Aggregates, since merged with Bardon Aggregates to form Aggregate Industries. The ballast traffic then declined and the branch was mothballed in 1998. However, EWS won a contract with Flexer Construction to move stone for cable-laying work from Meldon to various locations in Somerset and Devon from January 1999; the discharge points included Crediton, Taunton, Newton Abbot, Exmouth Junction, Goodrington, Plymouth Friary and Keyham. That traffic ended abruptly in 2000 when Flexer went into receivership. But Meldon survived: ballast trains operated again in 2001/02 and from 2004 onwards, serving various destinations including Westbury, Hinksey, Taunton and St Blazey.

A welcome rail freight development in Cornwall was the first trainload of sand derived from china clay waste from Burngullow to Bow in November 2005. Worked in two portions from Burngullow as far as Newton Abbot (Hackney Yard) and comprising JGA or HIA hopper wagons hauled by a Freightliner Heavy Haul Class 66, the service switched its destination to Angerstein Wharf and ran approximately once a fortnight during 2007. Flows of secondary aggregates such as this may become more widespread in future as restrictions on stone quarrying begin to bite.

●

The former station goods yard at Wool, Dorset, gained a new lease of life in 2000 when EWS won a contract with Aggregate Industries to move sand from the non-rail-connected Warmwell Quarry to Neasden, using PGA hopper wagons redeployed from the Mendips. In 2006 EWS lost this contract to Freightliner Heavy Haul, but in 2007 the company gained an additional flow from Wool to Watford Junction.

●

Until the 1990s rail-borne aggregates traffic in South Wales was mainly railway ballast. The

Nos 25225 and 45077 approach Cowley Bridge Junction, Exeter, with a trainload of ZJV 'Mermaid' side-tipping ballast wagons from Meldon Quarry on 14 May 1979.
Tom Heavyside

Above **Passing Cardiff Pengam Freightliner terminal on 28 August 1998 is Mirrlees-engined Class 37 No 37903 with the 1045 slag train from Llanwern to Cardiff Docks.**

Left **Class 58s were never common in South Wales but did appear on stone trains. No 58049 positions empty PGA hoppers in the former A. J. Williams coal loading siding at Cwmbargoed on 28 August 1998, ready to be loaded with gritstone for Hayes.**

ballast loading points at Tintern, Craig-y-Nos and Penderyn were closed by the early 1980s, but the ARC quarry at Machen on the former Bedwas branch near Newport continued to produce trainloads of ballast throughout the 1990s and into the 21st century. In 1987 Machen also dispatched trains to Allington for the construction industry, a foretaste of more regular commercial movements from Machen a decade later.

EWS in its early years was keen to tap into new markets, and its growth areas in the late 1990s included movements of water-cooled blast furnace slag for the construction industry. In 1998 EWS signed two contracts with Cambrian Stone, a joint venture between British Steel and Tarmac, to move 40,000 tonnes of slag from Port Talbot to Godstone for work at Gatwick Airport and 1 million tonnes of slag from Llanwern to Cardiff Docks for use at Tremorfa water treatment works.

EWS also established several loading points for high-value abrasive gritstone, used as a final dressing on road surfaces, from South Wales quarries. By summer 1998 Neath Abbey Wharf was loading stone from Gilfach Quarry for RMC, the former coal railhead at Cwmbargoed was loading stone from Gelligaer Quarry for Tarmac as well as from Hafod for Redland, the coal railhead at Cwmgwrach was loading stone from Cwm Nant Lleici Quarry for Bardon, and Machen was loading stone from Craig-yr-Hesg Quarry for ARC.

In 1999 Jersey Marine, near Neath, became a Bardon loading point with trains to Thorney Mill and Angerstein Wharf, and a new loading point was established on the approach to Newport Docks for gritstone to Radlett and Elstow. By 2001 two further locations in South Wales and neighbouring Herefordshire were added to the list: Tower Colliery for various flows operated by Mendip Rail, including stone from the formerly rail-connected quarry at Penderyn, and Hereford for Tarmac traffic to Hayes & Harlington and Hothfield.

In 2003 Tarmac received a Freight Facilities Grant of nearly £500,000 to establish a new loading point at Moreton-on-Lugg, which replaced Hereford in the following year. EWS operated trains from Moreton-on-Lugg to Hayes and Hothfield using HGA hoppers – cut-down ZFA 'Gunnell' infrastructure wagons that ironically had begun life as PGA aggregate hoppers in the early 1970s. Freightliner Heavy Haul used Moreton-on-Lugg as a loading point for trains to Bury and Harlow Mill.

Further developments in South Wales in the early 2000s included the use of Lafarge's self-discharge train on traffic from Cardiff Docks. Both Tower and Machen forwarded trains to Westbury for onward delivery to various railheads in the South East. Freightliner Heavy Haul took over the haulage of all Bardon trains in 2006, having already run a few trains from Jersey Marine to Burngullow in the previous year. The loading point for Bardon stone was switched from Jersey Marine to Neath Abbey Wharf in late 2006, and new destinations served from Neath in 2007 were Theale and Tavistock Junction Yard.

South East

Although the construction industry in London and the South East has had to look increasingly to other regions for its aggregate supplies, it also consumes large volumes of sea-dredged sand and gravel distributed from wharves in the Thames estuary, as well as small amounts of land-won sand and gravel from remaining pits in the Home Counties.

In the late 1960s BR ran trainloads of land-won sand from Southminster and Marks Tey to the former coal drops at Mile End, between Stratford and London Liverpool Street. The sand was carried in former ironstone hopper wagons, with a daily schedule of two 22-wagon trains from Southminster and two 24-wagon trains from Marks Tey. The Southminster flow ceased in 1978, while BR continued to run a daily train from Marks Tey to Mile End until the early 1990s, with HJV ex-ironstone hoppers having given way to air-braked stock in the late 1980s.

After the closure of Mile End, the loading point at Marks Tey remained in use for traffic to the Tarmac terminal at Hayes. EWS later introduced trains from Marks Tey to West Drayton and Crawley, as well as a short-term flow to Colnbrook for the building of Terminal 5 at Heathrow Airport. Various different wagon types have appeared on the Marks Tey traffic, latterly including EWS's HOA bogie hoppers.

Sand from Fen Drayton kept a 12-mile stretch of the former Cambridge to St Ives branch in use after its closure to passengers in 1970. A daily train ran from Fen Drayton to King's Cross Goods, with a second service operating up to three days a week to Allington. The King's Cross train continued running in the 1980s, still using re-bodied vacuum-braked HTV hoppers until their place was taken by air-braked PBA bogie hoppers in 1988. The train stopped running altogether in 1992, a victim of Trainload Freight's weeding out of unprofitable flows.

In West Sussex a short-distance but intensive operation conveyed roughly 500,000 tonnes a year of land-won gravel from Lavant, on the stub of the

Above A cluster of aggregates and cement terminals was located at King's Cross Goods, where pilot locomotive No 08670 is pictured shunting HTV hopper wagons from the Fen Drayton sand train on 28 October 1987. The site has since been transformed by Channel Tunnel Rail Link construction works.

Left No 73121 *Croydon 1883-1983* departs from Lavant with 6J38, the 1238 service to Drayton, on 18 August 1987. A tripper system at Lavant enabled the whole train to be loaded in a matter of minutes.

former Midhurst branch, to a processing plant at Drayton, just east of Chichester. The use of rail was a condition of the planning permission for the quarry, given the unsuitable nature of the roads in Chichester. The flow used a unique fleet of 11 side-discharge wagons, built in 1971 and later coded PHA. Although the Lavant branch was not electrified, the usual haulage for the six daily return trips in the 1980s was a Class 73 electro-diesel locomotive. The operation ceased in 1991.

A similarly intensive service operated until the 1970s carrying shingle from Lydd to Ashford,

Nos 33049 and 33046 shunt empty PHA hoppers at Salfords on 27 August 1987 before continuing their journey with 7Y94, the 1000 from Purley to Cliffe.

The compact Tarmac Topmix terminal at Paddington with its mobile unloader is pictured on 17 February 1993. The train locomotive is No 60039. The empty hoppers will return to Angerstein Wharf via the Greenford loop in order to avoid a reversal at Acton.

Allington and Merstham, with a schedule of six daily departures from Lydd.

Sea-dredged aggregate has been a growth area for rail freight in the London area in the last 40 years. Between 1968 and 1971 two fleets of air-braked bogie hopper wagons, later coded PHA (and subsequently JHA), were introduced on new flows for Murphy (later Marcon) from Angerstein Wharf and for Marinex (later Brett) from Cliffe, both on the south bank of the Thames estuary. BR introduced block trains from Angerstein Wharf to several depots in the London area and from Cliffe to Purley and Salfords. An unusual feature of the Murphy wagons was that they were designed for discharge by a lorry-mounted mobile conveyor, so that the receiving terminals did not have to be equipped with a hopper discharge pit.

Ten further wagons were added to the Marcon fleet in 1983. In the following year Marcon transferred its loading operation to the Brett terminal at Cliffe, but reverted to using its own facility at Angerstein Wharf in 1988. At that time Marcon ran up to two trains a day, each serving one of its terminals at Battersea, Park Royal, Paddington or King's Cross as required.

Under Mainline Freight management, the Marcon and Brett operations continued but with Luton Limbury Road as an additional destination served from Angerstein Wharf. EWS later accepted a larger stake in the Marcon operation by purchasing the company's fleet of 35 JHA hopper wagons, subsequently re-coded HLA, and two mobile unloaders. By 2002 the Brett traffic was no longer running to Salfords but additional flows

No 33040 rounds the curve from Hawkesbury Street Junction to Dover Town Yard with a minestone train from Snowdown to Sevington on 22 August 1989. Behind the locomotive is one of the YTX 'Queen Mary' brake-vans that allowed these trains to reverse out of Sevington sidings.

wagons in 1984. BR ran trains from Newhaven to Tolworth until 1989 and to Crawley in 1992. The Crawley flow resumed in 1994 but the revival was short-lived and the wagons were later transferred to the RMC fleet operating out of Peak Forest.

The rail connection to the long-closed Snowdown Colliery, Kent, made a comeback in the late 1980s when BR moved regular trainloads of minestone to Sevington for the building of the Channel Tunnel. This traffic used Tiger-owned PXA open box wagons and, in order to facilitate reversing movements, a small pool of refurbished YTX bogie brake-vans of Southern Railway vintage.

In the 1990s Grain in North Kent became a rail loading point for granite from the Foster Yeoman quarry at Glensanda, near Oban. Much of that traffic has been ballast for railway use, but regular supplies for the construction industry have operated to Crawley, using JUA open box wagons, and Grain has also forwarded granite for specific construction projects – notably Croydon Tramlink in 1998 and the Channel Tunnel Rail Link in 1999. At the time of writing GB Railfreight hauls ballast trains from Grain to Tonbridge and Ferme Park, while EWS serves the Network Rail virtual quarry at Hoo Junction.

Recycled aggregates made a modest but significant entry into the rail freight market in the early 2000s. Among the flows operated by EWS in South East England have been Purley to Sevington and Appleford to West Drayton, Allington and Ardingly. In 2007 GB Railfreight carried 10,000 tonnes of spent ballast from Acton to Parkeston, possibly paving the way for other similar flows.

were operating from Cliffe to Crawley and Battersea, both using railway-owned MBA box wagons. Meanwhile the Angerstein Wharf to King's Cross service was diverted to St Pancras from early 2005 as a result of Channel Tunnel Rail Link works.

The ARC terminal at Dagenham started forwarding sea-dredged aggregates in 1997, using two-axle PGA wagons that had previously operated out of the Mendips. The destinations served from Dagenham included Acton, West Drayton, Brentford and, later, Theale. A further new loading point on the north bank of the Thames in 2007 was West Thurrock, forwarding traffic to West Drayton.

A small-scale flow of sea-dredged aggregates operated out of Newhaven on the Sussex coast. This flow benefited from the introduction of a small fleet of PHA (later JHA) bogie hopper

Leicestershire

A cluster of granite quarries in Leicestershire has provided increasing volumes of rail freight since the early 1970s, serving a wide range of receiving depots in the South East, East Anglia and the West Midlands.

AGGREGATES

A new rail loading facility for the Redland quarry at Mountsorrel was commissioned in 1977, partly funded by a £1.1 million Section 8 Grant and enabling a gradual expansion of services. Redland acquired a fleet of air-braked PGA hopper wagons from 1978 onwards and put them to use on flows to Radlett, Elstow, Kennett, Norwich Trowse, Barham and Tallington. The Radlett depot was unique among roadstone terminals in being built on a continuous loop of track, similar to the 'merry-go-round' system adopted at many power stations. Mountsorrel also forwarded ballast to various locations such as York, Barnetby and Hitchin.

Redland's greatest rail freight innovation was its introduction of the Self Discharge Train (SDT) in 1988. The SDT comprised up to four units of ten semi-permanently coupled PGA (later PHA) hopper wagons, with each unit having a continuous conveyor belt at solebar level on to which the hoppers discharged; this conveyor belt was connected to an adjustable boom conveyor mounted on a special bogie wagon at one end of the

With 42 Redland PGA hoppers in tow, No 56065 passes the Midland Railway box at Melton Mowbray with 6C31, the 0858 from Mountsorrel to Radlett, on 30 June 1989.

train. The SDT enabled Redland to serve terminals without any kind of discharge equipment; all that was needed was a suitable area of hard standing next to the discharge siding. By 1990 the SDT was scheduled to serve Banbury, Cricklewood, Langley Junction (Stevenage), Chesterton Junction, Broxbourne and Chelmsford.

Under EWS management, the traffic volume out of Mountsorrel continued to grow. In early 2002 EWS signed a seven-year contract with Redland's successor Lafarge for between 24 and 35 trains a week to a total of ten distribution depots. A high-profile addition to the network in that year was Boston Docks, partly funded by a Freight Facilities Grant of just over £150,000. Another new destination was Small Heath. However, EWS did not have the monopoly of the Lafarge business: during 2005 Freightliner Heavy Haul launched a service from Mountsorrel to Luton Limbury Road, using Heavy Haul MJA box wagons. Ballast traffic from Mountsorrel was divided between EWS, Freightliner Heavy Haul and GB Railfreight.

The former goods yard at Loughborough was a loading point for railway ballast until the late 1980s. After the ballast traffic ended, BR conveyed a weekly train of granite from Loughborough to Ardingly, but this had ceased by the early 1990s.

Redland stone sample programme, August 1990

Code	Dep	Days	From	To
6E57	0225	TThFO	Mountsorrel	Langley
6L57	0225	WO	Mountsorrel	Chesterton Junction
6C39	0350	FO	Mountsorrel	Cricklewood
6V33	0354	MO	Mountsorrel	Banbury
6L23	0728	WThFO	Mountsorrel	Barham/Trowse
6C31	0834	SX	Mountsorrel	Radlett
6C33	1854	MTThO	Mountsorrel	Elstow
6L57	1924	ThO	Mountsorrel	Broxbourne
6L57	1924	FO	Mountsorrel	Colchester

An empty Redland self-discharge train returning to Mountsorrel passes Cossington on 23 April 1990, hauled by faded 'large logo'-liveried No 56103.

No 66043 slows to a halt beside the 1874-built GNR box at West Street Junction, Boston, with the Lafarge self-discharge train forming the 0719 departure from Mountsorrel on 7 June 2005.

AGGREGATES

Tiphook hopper wagons were used on Tarmac traffic from Cliffe Hill and Marks Tey. No 56063 shunts the stone terminal at Luton Limbury Road on 3 August 1990 after working 6C70, the 2147 from Cliffe Hill.

Trainload deliveries of Tarmac stone from Cliffe Hill to Hayes & Harlington started as long ago as 1966, using railway-owned flat-bottomed wagons for which a tippler installation was provided at Hayes. In 1977 Tarmac secured a £500,000 Section 8 Grant to renew the handling facilities at Cliffe Hill and Hayes, and in 1979 the company replaced the ageing railway-owned tipplers with air-braked PGA hopper wagons. Cliffe Hill was also an important supplier of railway ballast, with trains operating to Tonbridge, Doncaster and Bescot in the mid-1980s.

The lineside loading terminal at Cliffe Hill was replaced by an improved terminal at Stud Farm, at the end of a short spur from Cliffe Hill, in the late 1980s. Alongside the existing flow to Hayes Tarmac introduced services to Hothfield and, on a short-term basis, to Luton Limbury Road and Eccles Road.

Stud Farm continued to provide healthy volumes of ballast and roadstone as EWS took over the UK's bulk rail freight operations in 1996. Under the new arrangements for ballast distribution, Stud Farm fed the Railtrack virtual quarries at Rugby, Bescot and Oxford Hinksey. In 2001 Freightliner Heavy Haul took a share of the business from Stud Farm, while in 2007 GB Railfreight launched new flows from Stud Farm to Bury St Edmunds and Marks Tey. However, EWS retained the long-standing flows to Hayes and Hothfield and introduced its new HOA bogie hopper wagons on these services.

Granite from Bardon Hill Quarry, also on the Coalville line, benefited from a new fleet of air-braked PHA (later JHA) hopper wagons in 1986. The wagons were used initially on services to Thorney Mill and Brentford. The quarry firm Bardon received a £1.5 million Section 8 Grant to build a new terminal at Angerstein Wharf in 1990, which would receive limestone from Merehead as well as granite from Bardon Hill.

Croft Quarry, on the Leicester to Nuneaton line, is another long-established railhead for granite. In 1986 BR and the quarry operator ECC introduced air-braked PGA hopper wagons on block trains from Croft to Bow, and from 1988 to the former coal depot at Bishops Stortford. The quarry also produced railway ballast for various destinations including Whitemoor and Leyton.

In 1994 the quarrying arm of ECC was de-merged from the parent company and became known as Camas, then Camas merged with Bardon in the late 1990s to become Aggregate Industries. EWS then won a seven-year contract with Aggregate Industries for flows from Bardon Hill, Croft and South Wales. In 1998 a new receiving terminal for Bardon traffic was built at Neasden with the support of a £1.9 million Freight Facilities Grant. Another terminal development was the closure of Bishops Stortford in favour of a much expanded facility at Harlow Mill, supported by a £2 million Freight Facilities Grant.

Aggregate Industries introduced a new fleet of 22 bogie JGA hopper wagons in 2005, fitted with

No 58038 departs from Bardon Hill after running round its train of PGA hoppers forming 6V76 from Cliffe Hill to Hayes on 30 October 1986.

low-track-force bogies to reduce wear and tear on the infrastructure and therefore incur lower charges from Network Rail. From 2006 the core roadstone traffic out of Bardon Hill and Croft switched from EWS to Freightliner Heavy Haul; however, EWS picked up new flows from Bardon Hill to Watford Junction and from Croft to Brierley Hill, using PGA hoppers and MBA box wagons respectively.

In addition to the regular flows, Bardon Hill has supplied stone for several specific construction projects. These operations have included boulders to Ferriby for sea defences on the Humber estuary, roadstone to Gascoigne Wood for upgrading the M62/A1 interchange at Ferrybridge, and ballast to Bury for track renewal on the Manchester Metrolink. The last two flows brought freight traffic back to the otherwise little-used stretch of line between Bardon Hill and Burton-on-Trent.

Derbyshire

The ICI quarry at Tunstead, on the former Midland Railway main line from Manchester to Derby, was already a major source of rail-borne limestone traffic well before the Second World War. At nationalisation BR inherited the operation of block trains from Tunstead to the ICI chemical plants in the Northwich area at Lostock and Winnington (Oakleigh), using a dedicated fleet of vacuum-braked 48-ton-capacity bogie hopper wagons, some of which dated back to 1936; ICI had opted for vacuum-braked rather than unfitted stock because of the steep gradients on the route. Construction of these wagons continued until the early 1950s, with the fleet eventually numbering 152 vehicles.

In the early 1970s BR operated up to six trains from Tunstead to the Northwich area each day from Monday to Saturday, plus three trains on Sundays. The 18-wagon trains were hauled by a single Class 25 locomotive, with banking assistance for the climb out of Tunstead. BR also conveyed a limited amount of roadstone from Tunstead at that time, with scheduled trains to Collyhurst Street, Thorpes Bridge Junction (Dean Lane) and Portwood.

In the 1980s ICI boosted its wagon fleet (now coded PHV) by acquiring 13 vehicles of a similar design, which had been made redundant from iron ore traffic between Bidston and Shotton. The reign of the single Class 25s ended in 1984, when the Tunstead bankers were withdrawn and double-headed Class 20s took sole charge of the trains, including the short-lived sub-class 20/3 variant with modified braking equipment. In late 1986 the Class 20s gave way to a mixture of single Class 47s – with banking assistance reinstated – and pairs of refurbished Class 37s, with the 37s becoming dominant after the summer of 1989.

No 25134 takes the former Midland Railway line through New Mills with 6F42, the ICI limestone train from Tunstead to Northwich, on 28 October 1982.

In January 1988 the use of ICI's PHV wagons was extended to a new short-distance flow of limestone from Tunstead to the ICI lime plant at Hindlow, following the end of quarrying at Hindlow. Despite covering a distance of just 9 miles, this flow was operationally complex with run-round movements at Peak Forest and Buxton. The PHVs also remained in use on the core Northwich operation and on roadstone flows to Collyhurst Street, Dean Lane and Bredbury – the latter terminal having replaced Portwood in 1987. The roadstone flows lasted until 1990, while the Hindlow operation went over to air-braked operation following the awarding of a £2.62 million Freight Facilities Grant for new JGA wagons and handling facilities in 1994. Without that grant, it is likely that the traffic would have passed to road.

Following the de-merger of ICI in the early 1990s, Tunstead Quarry and the remaining fleet of ex-ICI hopper wagons (now coded JGV) passed to Buxton Lime Industries, while the Northwich chemical plants reverted to the earlier name of Brunner Mond. The limestone movements carried on as before thanks to the signing of a long-term contract between the two parties. However, the operation of vacuum-braked wagons had long become an anachronism. Options for haulage of the Brunner Mond trains had become limited because all diesel locomotives built after the 1960s had been equipped for air brake operation only. This meant having to use pairs of ageing Class 37 locomotives on the Brunner Mond trains when most other limestone trains out of the Peak District had gone over to Class 60 haulage. And although the traffic ran in full trainloads, the discharge arrangements at both Lostock and Winnington required a lot of shunting, leading to poor wagon turnaround times by modern standards.

The decision to phase out the JGV wagons was finally taken in 1997. The last loaded workings

Trainload Construction-liveried No 60085 *Axe Edge* heads south from Great Rocks Junction with limestone from Tunstead to Hindlow on 22 July 1994.

took place on 28 December of that year and the wagons were de-registered from the main-line fleet three days later. As a stop-gap Brunner Mond kept the Tunstead to Northwich flow ticking over by hiring a fleet of 112 two-axle air-braked hopper wagons (PGA) from the leasing company CAIB. These wagons had been built between 1979 and 1981 and had been used for limestone traffic from the Mendips until replaced by higher-capacity bogie vehicles. The fact that the PGAs were superseded in the Mendips after less than 20 years makes the longevity of the JGVs seem all the more impressive!

The use of PGAs brought some immediate benefits, as did the introduction of a revised train plan. Because the PGAs had a better payload-to-tare-weight ratio than the JGVs, the payload per train was increased from 1,100 tonnes (in 24 JGVs) to 1,350 tonnes (in 36 PGAs) without increasing the gross weight of the train. This in turn allowed a reduction from 17 to 14 trains per week. Whereas the trainloads of JGVs had always served a single destination – either Lostock or Winnington – the train plan for the PGAs included the option of split deliveries, enabling both locations to receive two deliveries a day. The reduction in wagon turnaround time from 48 to 36 hours meant that the number of train sets in operation could be reduced from four to three.

Looking to the longer term, Brunner Mond

secured a £6.1 million Freight Facilities Grant in September 1999 towards the £9 million cost of new rolling-stock and improved terminal facilities. This was the biggest ever Freight Facilities Grant awarded in England. The wagon fleet comprised 27 102-tonne bogie hoppers, coded JEA, which were delivered by the end of 2000. EWS then introduced a new train plan, with up to 11 loaded trains spread across a seven-day week. The terminal facilities at Lostock and Winnington were hugely simplified, with just a single discharge siding, run-round loop and two wagon maintenance sidings at each location.

Alongside the Brunner Mond traffic, Buxton Lime Industries developed other rail-borne flows, including the return of roadstone traffic to Bredbury in 1998 and the launch of seasonal (August to January) sugar stone trains to Brandon (for British Sugar Wissington), Bury St Edmunds, Norwich (for Cantley) and Ipswich in the same year. The Tarmac receiving terminal at Pendleton (Agecroft) re-opened in 2000 for trainload deliveries from Tunstead. Buxton Lime Industries also continued to forward trainloads of limestone to the flue gas desulphurisation plant at Drax, now hauled by EWS but still using the ex-National Power Class 59 and JHA hopper wagons introduced in 1993, and to Ratcliffe using a mixture of Buxton Lime Industries JGA and ex-Tiphook KPA (formerly PIA) bogie hopper wagons.

Peak District stone train plan, May 1972

Code	Dep	Days	From	To
6J30	0430	SX	Tunstead	Thorpes Bridge Junction
6J31	0513	SX	Tunstead	Collyhurst Street
6F47	0556	SX	Tunstead	Widnes
6F40	0710	EWD	Tunstead	Wallerscote
6F41	0920	EWD	Tunstead	Oakleigh
6J32	1135	SX	Tunstead	Thorpes Bridge Junction
6J34	1220	SX	Tunstead	Collyhurst Street
6F42	1324	EWD	Tunstead	Northwich
6F42	1325	SuO	Tunstead	Northwich
6J33	1435	SX	Tunstead	Thorpes Bridge Junction
6F43	1522	EWD	Tunstead	Oakleigh
6F43	1522	SuO	Tunstead	Oakleigh
6E46	1420	SX	Hindlow	Lackenby
6F44	1724	SuO	Tunstead	Northwich
8E57	1811	SX	Peak Forest	Healey Mills
6F44	1910	EWD	Tunstead	Wallerscote
9F81	2105	SX	Peak Forest	Dee Marsh Junction
6F45	2115	EWD	Tunstead	Wallerscote or Northwich
8E38	2238	WFO	Peak Forest	Wilton

Peak District stone train plan, September 1995

Code	Dep	Days	From	To
6B10	0212	SO	Peak Forest	Bletchley
6J46	0346	EWD	Peak Forest	Hope Street
7F48	0446	SX	Tunstead	Northwich
6H20	0520	TWFO	Tunstead	Hindlow
6M85	0528	MThO	Tunstead	Ratcliffe
6E17	0628	SX	Peak Forest	Leeds Balm Road
6E56	0637	SX	Tunstead	Drax
7F48	0730	SO	Tunstead	Northwich
6H24	0820	SO	Tunstead	Hindlow
7F49	0844	SuO	Tunstead	Northwich
6B10	0957	TWThO	Peak Forest	Bletchley
7F49	1100	MWFO	Tunstead	Oakleigh
6E68	1234	ThO	Peak Forest	Selby
6H22	1330	TWFO	Tunstead	Hindlow
6M42	1400	TSX	Peak Forest	Washwood Heath
6H22	1425	MThO	Tunstead	Hindlow
7F50	1500	SO	Tunstead	Oakleigh
7F50	1624	SX	Tunstead	Oakleigh
7F50	1630	SuO	Tunstead	Oakleigh

Comprising a mixture of white- and green-liveried HIA hopper wagons, the 1258 limestone empties from Drax to Barrow Hill passes Whitley Bridge Junction on 19 July 2007 behind No 66606.

The building of the second runway at Manchester Airport brought a substantial flow from Tunstead and from neighbouring Dove Holes, with a total of 1.4 million tonnes of limestone conveyed between December 1997 and 1999. Manchester Airport Authority obtained a Section 139 Grant to build a 1.3-mile branch and receiving terminal near Manchester Airport station for the traffic. The train plan for 1998 comprised one train a day from each of Tunstead and Dove Holes, using mainly hired ex-Tiphook hopper wagons.

The seasonal sugar stone traffic from Tunstead to East Anglia continued into the 21st century, peaking at just over 100,000 tonnes in the 2003/04 season. However, by 2007 the traffic was operating only to Norwich. The flue gas desulphurisation flows to Ratcliffe and Drax passed to Freightliner Heavy Haul in 2005 and 2006 respectively, while the new flue gas desulphurisation plant at West Burton brought an additional flow from Tunstead in 2003, hauled initially by EWS but later by Freightliner Heavy Haul.

●

The Tarmac quarry at Topley Pike produced regular trainload traffic in the 1970s and 1980s. The company introduced air-braked PGA hopper wagons on its flows to Pendleton and Widnes in 1974. In order to maximise the payload per train, Tarmac pooled its wagon fleet with that belonging to Peakstone, the subsidiary of Ready Mixed Concrete (RMC), which now owned Dove Holes

Quarry. A single 38-wagon train, known locally at the time as 'the Big Train', completed two out and back journeys each day, serving either Pendleton or Widnes in the morning and the Peakstone depot at Salford Hope Street in the afternoon. Regular traffic from Topley Pike ceased in 1987 when planning permission to extend the quarrying was withheld. However, the sidings at Topley Pike remained in use as a maintenance location for the Tarmac wagon fleet.

The Staveley quarry at Dove Holes (Peak Forest) was already a source of rail freight in the early BR era. However, traffic grew rapidly from the 1970s onwards, with its new owner RMC keen to develop trainload flows of roadstone to Manchester, Birmingham and other strategic locations. The company's first regular use of air-braked wagons was the traffic to Salford Hope Street mentioned above. Other flows from Dove Holes relied on elderly vacuum-braked stock – HTV former coal hoppers for ad hoc movements to Selby and Ely, and MSV former ironstone tipplers for scheduled trains to Leeds Balm Road and Bletchley.

In 1987 RMC received the first of several batches of air-braked bogie hopper wagons, coded PHA (later JGA). They were put to use on a new flow from Dove Holes to Washwood Heath, as well as covering a weekly train of granite from Penmaenmawr to Salford Hope Street. The vacuum-braked stock on trains to Ely, Bletchley and Leeds lasted until 1989, after which Ely and Bletchley used Peakstone/RMC air-braked

Above The stone terminal at Leeds Balm Road continued to receive limestone in vacuum-braked wagons until the late 1980s. Nos 37215 and 31299 arrive at Balm Road with loaded MSV wagons on 29 August 1986, forming 8L18, the 1345 departure from Peak Forest. The site of the stone terminal is now occupied by Leeds Midland Road maintenance depot.

Right No 37259 shunts PGA hoppers at Dove Holes Quarry on 12 April 1988, ready to form the afternoon departure from Peak Forest to Salford Hope Street. On the left are some of the few vacuum-braked HTV hoppers that remained in revenue use at that time.

Right RMC introduced several batches of bogie hopper wagons, some with flat bodysides and others with a curved profile as can be seen in this photograph. No 60026 enters Manchester Victoria station with 6H60, the 0840 empties from Hope Street to Peak Forest, on 12 August 1991.

hoppers, and Leeds Balm Road – which did not have a hopper discharge facility – used flat-bottomed open wagons hired from Procor.

RMC later expanded its fleet of JGA wagons by ordering new stock and by acquiring the 1984-built Hall Aggregates hoppers that used to work out of Newhaven. A new hopper discharge terminal at Leeds Stourton enabled the closure of Balm Road in 1998, so that RMC could standardise on hopper wagons for all its regular flows. By the end of that year RMC was operating three rakes of JGAs, each comprising between 25 and 28 vehicles and covering a weekly schedule of four or five trains to each of Salford, Leeds and Bletchley, plus one or two trains to each of Washwood Heath, Selby and Ely. RMC also supplied limestone to Manchester Airport jointly with Buxton Lime Industries, as described above.

The first years of the 21st century brought a number of new flows from Dove Holes. The former steel terminal at Brierley Hill received its first stone from Dove Holes in 2000, using MBA bogie box wagons for discharge by mechanical grab. In 2002 EWS ran trainloads of MBAs from Dove Holes to three East Anglian destinations: Eccles Road for A11 road upgrading works, Brandon for runway improvements at RAF Lakenheath, and Peterborough for the building of a new furniture warehouse.

In 2003 EWS signed a seven-year contract with RMC (soon to become part of the Cemex group) for limestone traffic to Salford, Leeds, Bletchley, Washwood Heath, Selby and Ely. It added a new flow of dry silo mortar to the Bletchley train, using 15 specially converted PCA wagons. In the same year EWS began a short-term flow from Dove Holes to Acton for the redevelopment of White City, using Mendip Rail hopper wagons. In 2007 EWS introduced Cemex-liveried HOA bogie hopper wagons on various flows from Dove Holes.

Meanwhile Freightliner Heavy Haul competed successfully for some RMC/Cemex traffic, including fixed-term movements to Wymondham and Eccles Road and longer-term flows to Hitchin and Attercliffe Road (Sheffield). However, the Hitchin and Attercliffe Road business switched to EWS in 2007, using the MBA wagons previously allocated to Drax-Northwich fly ash traffic.

The Lafarge (formerly Redland) quarry at Dowlow, adjacent to Hindlow on the former LNWR line south of Buxton, started sending out limestone by rail in 1997, with a fixed-term flow to Ashburys for the M60 motorway extension on the east side of Manchester. EWS supplied MEA open box wagons for this traffic. The operation was successful and in October 1998 Lafarge received a £590,000 Freight Facilities Grant to make its Dowlow and Ashburys terminals more permanent. In late 1999 EWS was running two daily trains from Dowlow to Ashburys. Lafarge later obtained a second grant for a new terminal at Northenden, on the site of the former Blue Circle cement depot, and sporadic deliveries to Northenden started in 2004.

Alongside the trains to Ashburys and Northenden, EWS gained long-distance limestone flows from Dowlow to Kennett and Barham. This traffic passed to Freightliner Heavy Haul in 2005. Further new business for Freightliner Heavy Haul included limestone from Dowlow to the flue gas desulphurisation plants at Cottam and Eggborough and to Garston for the construction industry. The flows to Kennett, Barham, Cottam and Eggborough all used HIA hopper wagons, while the Garston traffic used MJA open box wagons. Freightliner Heavy Haul also used MJAs on a trial movement to Ferrybridge power station in 2006.

●

The 9-mile Wirksworth branch remained in use for limestone traffic long after its 1947 closure to passengers. The last flow on the branch was seasonal sugar stone for South Lynn, which was loaded in the top yard and conveyed in vacuum-braked HTV hoppers. This service ceased in 1990. Fortunately much of the railway infrastructure was left in place and the branch now hosts a heritage operation known as the Ecclesbourne Valley Railway.

●

The Steetley limestone quarry at Whitwell, close to the Derbyshire-Nottinghamshire boundary, re-opened to rail traffic in 1989. After dispatching trains to Wednesbury for a trial period, BR introduced a three-times-weekly service from Whitwell to Witton, in the northern suburbs of

AGGREGATES

Displaced from its Midland Main Line passenger duties by InterCity 125s, 'Peak' No 45146 leaves Wirksworth with 8P07 to Derby St Marys on 29 October 1986, conveying sugar stone for South Lynn.

A short-lived limestone flow operated from Whitwell to Witton, using Tiger POA box wagons. No 56058 approaches its destination with the 6Z61 empties from Toton to Whitwell on 17 August 1990.

Whistling past Leek Brook Junction box on 10 April 1984 is No 40174, in charge of the 7L82 stone train from Caldon Low to Witton. The load comprises MSV wagons and one low-sided MTV vehicle.

Birmingham, using hired POA flat-bottomed wagons. Loading and discharge were carried out by mechanical grab. The flow lasted only a few years and the sidings at Whitwell then returned to disuse.

●

In Staffordshire, the Tarmac quarry at Caldon Low produced regular limestone traffic to Witton, with three weekly trainloads operating in the 1980s. The flow used railway-owned open box wagons of various types including MDV, MSV and MTV. Because of the gradients each loaded train had to be worked in two portions from Caldon Low to Leek Brook Junction, which was also the run-round location for sand trains from Oakamoor. The traffic ceased in February 1989, five months after the end of sand traffic from Oakamoor and therefore bringing the complete closure of the 18-mile route from Caldon Low to Stoke-on-Trent. Rumours of a possible revival for Caldon Low were widespread in the 1990s and a train path for traffic to Eccles Road even appeared in the working timetable for 1999. However, that revival was not to be.

Northern England and North Wales

The 22-mile Redmire branch in Wensleydale survived to gain a new lease of life in 1977 with a daily train of limestone from Redmire to the British Steel blast furnace at Redcar. Although the trains consisted of air-braked PGA hopper wagons, they conveyed a brake-van at the rear so that the guard could close the gates at several unstaffed level crossings on the line. Following British Steel's decision to source its limestone from Hardendale (Shap), the last loaded departure from Redmire ran on 18 December 1992. However, the Redmire branch did not die: it re-opened for occasional military trains in 1996 and was later leased by Network Rail to the Wensleydale Railway Company, who restored passenger services in 2003.

Thrislington Quarry in County Durham produced flows of magnesium limestone to steelworks and other industrial destinations. A local flow of lime and dolime (calcined dolomite) operated until 2004 from Thrislington to the

Steetley magnesia works at Hartlepool, using railway-owned CHO/CHP covered hopper wagons until the early 1980s and private-owner PAA/PAB covered hopper wagons thereafter. Another long-standing destination for lime and dolime was Ravenscraig steelworks, but that business ceased with the closure of Ravenscraig. However, in 2000 EWS gained a new flow of containerised lime from Thrislington to the Corus plant at Port Talbot, using FCA intermodal wagons.

The quarries of County Durham also produced magnesium limestone for agricultural use. In the 1970s this traffic ran from Thrislington and Raisby Hill to many destinations in Scotland, using railway-owned mineral and hopper wagons. The number of destinations declined in the 1980s, partly because of cutbacks in wagonload trip workings to station goods yards and partly because it was hard to justify investment in new rolling-stock given the seasonal nature of the traffic. However, in 1985 W. & M. Thompson introduced a fleet of five 60-tonne PTA (later JQA) bogie side-tipping wagons to carry agricultural lime from Ferryhill to Montrose. That flow continued until the early 2000s. EWS trialled agricultural lime traffic to other destinations, including a delivery to Fearn on the Far North line in MEA box wagons, but no long-term flows became established.

Steelworks slag for the construction industry produced a small amount of rail traffic in the early 2000s. Freightliner Heavy Haul hauled trainloads of slag from Port Clarence to Chesterton Junction in 2003/04 and from Middlesbrough to Eastleigh in 2008. EWS ran a trial movement of slag from Scunthorpe to Pendleton in 2004, using JGA hopper wagons from the Rylstone-Hull circuit.

●

Expansion at Tilcon's Rylstone (Swinden) Quarry in the early 1970s assured a reprieve for the Grassington branch, which had closed to regular passenger traffic in 1930 and to general freight in 1969. Tilcon acquired a fleet of 33 PGA hopper wagons and contracted BR to move up to 500,000 tonnes of limestone a year from Rylstone to receiving depots at Hull Dairycoates and Leeds Marsh Lane. Intensive diagramming enabled a single set of wagons to cover two out-and-back journeys in a 24-hour period.

AGGREGATES

Traffic from Rylstone received a further boost in 1994 when Tilcon received a £3.1 million Freight Facilities Grant for 30 air-braked JGA hopper wagons and a new receiving terminal at Leeds Hunslet East, not far from the existing Marsh Lane facility. Tilcon renewed its contract with BR for a further 10-year period, although the traffic was soon transferred to EWS as privatisation took effect.

The Rylstone schedule in 1998 comprised two trains each weekday, with one train destined for either Hull Dairycoates or Leeds Marsh Lane and the other destined for Hunslet East. In the same year EWS launched a new flow from Rylstone to Dewsbury. This traffic was notable for its low start-up costs, with the wagons being discharged across the boundary fence by a mechanical shovel from an existing track forming the run-round loop for Dewsbury cement terminal. The first trains comprised ZCA and ZAA infrastructure wagons, later giving way to MEA open box wagons.

Right No 60031 *Ben Lui* positions its rake of empty PGA wagons under the loader at Redmire after forming 6N53, the 0925 departure from Redcar, on 14 March 1992.

Below The 6P62 train conveying empty Steetley hoppers from Hartlepool to Thrislington arrives at Ferryhill on 16 July 1986, headed by No 47307. On the far left is the loading point for agricultural lime to Scotland.

A rake of the original Tilcon two-axle air-braked hopper wagons is hauled past Skipton station on 25 August 1993 by Class 60 No 60005 *Skiddaw*. The train is 6E63, the 1016 from Rylstone to Leeds Marsh Lane.

Another new destination served from Rylstone was Heck, again using MEA wagons.

In 2002 Tilcon's successor Tarmac Northern received a £1.3 million grant from the Strategic Rail Authority for upgrading the Hunslet East terminal. EWS also continued to serve Hull and Dewsbury and ran a weekly 'as required' service from Rylstone to Redcar for Corus. In 2006 GB Railfreight hauled a short-term flow from Rylstone to Bury St Edmunds, using JNA open box wagons.

●

Three rail-connected quarries flank a 4-mile stretch of the West Coast Main Line at Shap. The southernmost site is Shap Summit, where RMC produces granite for use as railway ballast. At the time of writing Freightliner Heavy Haul operates ballast trains from Shap Summit to Carlisle and Crewe. One mile north of Shap Summit is the Hardendale (Shapfell) complex, operated by Corus and comprising a limestone quarry and lime works. The long-standing lime traffic from Hardendale to Lackenby was joined in 1993 by a flow of limestone to Redcar, replacing the previous flow from Redmire. After the change of source the limestone continued to be carried in British Steel PGA hopper wagons, which later passed into EWS ownership and were re-coded HGA. The third stone loading point at Shap is the Hanson quarry at Harrison's Sidings (Shap Beck). EWS launched

a twice-weekly train of limestone dust from Harrison's Sidings to Redcar in 1999, using hooded HFA hopper wagons redeployed from coal traffic. The Hanson quarry has also produced an intermittent flow of limestone to Ashton-in-Makerfield for the construction industry, using MEA wagons.

●

Penmaenmawr Quarry on the North Wales coast has been a regular source of railway ballast for many decades, supplying various yards in North West England from where the ballast is distributed to work sites. In the late 1980s scheduled ballast trains ran from Penmaenmawr to Crewe, Carnforth, Bamber Bridge and Ashburys. A major shake-up of services from Penmaenmawr took place in 1998 when Railtrack established its network of virtual quarries and local distribution centres (see the next section). The previous pattern of up to three daily trains to different locations was replaced by a single daily departure for either Guide Bridge or Carnforth. This train was later amended to run to Crewe Basford Hall Yard and its haulage passed from EWS to Freightliner Heavy Haul in 2001. At the time of writing the daily train is supplemented by a second working when required.

Penmaenmawr has produced intermittent flows of stone for the construction industry. In the 1970s

BR ran a daily service from Penmaenmawr to either Sandhills (Liverpool) or Salford Hope Street, and in the late 1980s the weekly train to Hope Street used RMC bogie hopper wagons normally based in the Peak District. In more recent years EWS has run trains from Penmaenmawr to Ashton-in-Makerfield and Tytherington, and Freightliner Heavy Haul has operated an occasional service to Chesterton Junction, Cambridge.

The slate tips of Blaenau Ffestiniog have the potential to produce a major rail freight flow, now that the construction industry has tax incentives for using recycled aggregates instead of quarried stone or gravel. Freightliner Heavy Haul ran a trial movement of slate waste from Blaenau Ffestiniog in November 2002, but at the time of writing the project is stuck in a funding impasse, with no one willing to foot the bill for upgrading the Conwy Valley line – for which estimates range between a modest £4 million and an incomprehensible £200 million. Unfortunately the Welsh Assembly turned down a grant application for the traffic in 2004 and matters are not helped by the opposition of some local people to the prospect of 'noisy trains'.

Railway ballast

Traditionally, ballast and other materials for railway use such as spoil, sleepers and rails were carried 'free on rail'. BR carried ballast from a large number of quarries and loading points to an even larger number of yards, from where the ballast was delivered as required to engineering possessions, ie to work sites where the railway was closed to normal traffic to allow re-ballasting and other engineering activity to take place.

The fact that ballast and other infrastructure materials were non-revenue-earning, or 'departmental', meant that they were a low priority for investment. The wagons were often cast-offs from the revenue-earning fleet and some unfitted vehicles, ie wagons with no continuous brake, were still in departmental use long after they had disappeared from revenue-earning freight flows. Likewise, motive power for ballast trains was often whatever was available on the day.

In 1994 the break-up of British Rail into units for privatisation brought a change in culture for infrastructure traffic. Trains of ballast and other materials were governed by contracts between Railtrack and the freight operators – initially Loadhaul, Mainline Freight and Transrail, later amalgamated into EWS. Possession trains required tripartite contracts between Railtrack, the freight operators and the 13 engineering companies that carried out the infrastructure work.

While the competition between the various engineering companies kept down the costs of the engineering work, the running of trains was another matter. Each engineering company was free to source its materials from wherever it wanted, and this often resulted in small quantities of traffic being ordered from many different locations. The overall planning of train

A train of 'Dogfish' ballast wagons from Penderyn heads towards Mountain Ash behind green-liveried Class 37 No 6913 on 25 May 1973. *Tom Heavyside*

Above No 40092 weaves past Chester No 2 box with 6F27, the 1013 Penmaenmawr to St Helens ballast working, on 13 August 1982.

Left No 25042 draws its train of empty ballast hoppers under the loader at Blodwell on 21 August 1985. It will form 7G25, the 1528 departure to Bescot. Ballast traffic from Blodwell ceased in 1988, leaving no further use for the 7-mile branch from Gobowen.

movements was complex. Therefore during 1997 a strategic review was carried out by EWS, Railtrack, the infrastructure engineering contractors and materials suppliers, to see how train operations could be made more efficient.

The outcome of the review was an agreement to concentrate the formation of possession trains on 16 'local distribution centres' (LDCs), to reduce the number of ballast sourcing points from more than 12 quarries to just three or four, to streamline the distribution of ballast through the creation of 'virtual quarries' associated with each LDC, and to rationalise the disposal of waste ballast by making train operations more efficient and by recycling the material at some of the LDCs. The virtual

AGGREGATES

	'Virtual quarries' and local distribution centres, January 1999	
Quarry	**Virtual quarry**	**Local distribution centre**
Cloburn (by road)	Carstairs	Mossend
		Millerhill
Mountsorrel	Tyne Yard	Tyne Yard
	Doncaster	Doncaster
	Toton	Toton
	Peterborough	Peterborough
Penmaenmawr	Carnforth	Carnforth
	Guide Bridge	Guide Bridge
Stud Farm	Bescot	Bescot
	Rugby	Rugby
	Hinksey	Hinksey
Machen	-	Newport
Glensanda (by sea)	Southampton	Eastleigh
	Westbury (via Southampton)	Westbury
	Purfleet	Temple Mills
	Grain	Hoo Junction

quarries, which were basically stockpiles of ballast at strategic railway locations, came into operation during 1998, with the network of other trains conveying materials to and from the LDCs falling into place during 1999. The initial network is shown in the accompanying table.

The setting up of virtual quarries and LDCs made it possible to carry the ballast in trainloads of 2,000 tonnes and above, leading to better use of traction and traincrew resources. Because the ballast was stockpiled at the virtual quarry, the wagons used for the first leg of the journey could be the open box type, releasing more specialised hopper wagons for use on possession trains. Railtrack hired a sizeable fleet of JNA and PNA open box wagons from CAIB to supplement those provided by EWS.

Meanwhile EWS set about modernising its own wagon fleet, which in 1997 still amounted to some 6,000 vehicles – comprising 4,000 open wagons for spoil and other materials, 1,200 hoppers for ballast, 500 flat wagons for rails and track panels, and 300 specialist vehicles such as well wagons, brake-vans and runner wagons. Roughly one-third of that fleet was vacuum-braked – more than 30 years after BR had adopted air brakes as standard.

The modernisation programme included the conversion of 300 ZCA 'Sea Urchin' open wagons from SPA plate wagons, 400 MHA box wagons using the underframes of redundant HAA and HEA coal hoppers, and 200 MTA low-sided spoil wagons using the underframes of redundant Shell tank wagons. EWS fitted American-style bogies to 400 'Salmon' sleeper carriers and ordered replacements for the 700-strong fleet of vacuum-braked 'Dogfish' ballast hoppers.

An important feature of new builds of ballast hoppers was the provision of remotely controlled power doors. Ten power-door discharge 'Autoballasters' were converted from KPA aggregate hoppers by Tiphook in 1996 and these were followed up by further orders. The Redland self-discharge train also started to appear on ballast duties, both for ballast drops in possessions and for ballast supply to some of the virtual quarries.

Following the 1997 review Railtrack and EWS signed a seven-year agreement for infrastructure traffic, accounting for between 15% and 20% of EWS's turnover. However, the supply network did not remain static: for example, in 1999 the entry point for ballast for Westbury was switched from Southampton to Grain, and in 2000 new virtual quarries were established at Crewe Basford Hall

Southampton Western Docks became one of the maritime railheads for railway ballast from Foster Yeoman's Glensanda Quarry. No 37274 enters the docks with 7B05, the 0907 trip working from Eastleigh Yard, on 20 July 1998. The train consists of YGB 'Seacow' wagons built in the 1970s.

and Carlisle Kingmoor, replacing Guide Bridge and Carnforth.

Meanwhile Freightliner ended EWS's monopoly of infrastructure traffic in 1999 as it signed an eight-year deal to provide traction for Railtrack's track construction and renewal programme. That contract effectively kick-started Freightliner's

Once the poor relation of rail freight, ballast traffic has benefited from more specialised technology in recent years. No 66509 shunts the ballast distribution system of the High Output Ballast Cleaner into Crewe Pre-Assembly Depot sidings ready for servicing on 30 August 2000.

Heavy Haul division, which would become a separate operating company within the Freightliner Group in 2001. It was the Railtrack contract that justified the order of Heavy Haul's first three Class 66 locomotives, paving the way for many further orders.

Initially Freightliner's duties included the haulage of specialised equipment owned either by Railtrack or by Railtrack's suppliers such as Jarvis and GTRM, including overhead line maintenance trains, the High Output Ballast Cleaner (HOBC), the Track Relaying Train and long-welded-rail trains. These operations involved an intensive

schedule that varied from week to week, in stark contrast to the predictability of Freightliner's intermodal services.

Freightliner then became the chosen operator for Crewe Regional Supply Centre, dovetailing conveniently with its existing base at Basford Hall Yard. Railtrack funded £3 million worth of improvements around the Basford Hall complex, including a new ballast stockpile, a spent ballast processing site and an additional stabling facility for infrastructure trains, including one specially lengthened siding to hold the HOBC.

Railtrack and its successor Network Rail awarded Freightliner Heavy Haul numerous further contracts, starting in 2001 with the scheduled movement of ballast from Shap to Carlisle; from Penmaenmawr to Crewe; from Mountsorrel to Doncaster; from Stud Farm to Crewe, Stewartby and Hinksey; from Bardon Hill to Crewe; from Southampton to Eastleigh and Westbury; and from Meldon to Hinksey. In 2004/05 Heavy Haul won the haulage contract for three additional high-output trains: a ballast-cleaner based at Reading, another based at Doncaster and a track renewal train based on the former Western Region.

GB Railfreight became a significant player in the infrastructure business when Network Rail appointed the company to operate its new yard at Whitemoor in 2004. By 2006 Whitemoor was handling up to 25 possession trains each weekend and around 10 scheduled departures during the week, with GB Railfreight and EWS sharing the haulage. GB Railfreight also won a three-year contract to move recycled ballast from Whitemoor to a new terminal at North Walsham.

In 2005 GB Railfreight (now First GBRf) won a major 10-year contract to supply rails, sleepers and ballast to engineering possessions on London Underground's sub-surface Metronet lines. This project included re-fettling Wellingborough yard as a stabling and stockpiling location, with First GBRf running trainloads of materials directly into the London Underground network during weekend engineering possessions. Other infrastructure flows operated by GB Railfreight have included sleepers between Peterborough and Taunton, ballast from Mountsorrel to Doncaster and Toton, and ballast from Grain to Tonbridge and Ferme Park.

Lime

Quicklime is calcium oxide; this is produced by the thermal decomposition of limestone, and is used in steel-making and in a number of other industrial processes.

Until the 1960s much industrial lime was carried in sheeted open wagons. However, in 1969 BR built 52 air-braked covered hopper wagons, based on the 'merry-go-round' coal design, which worked block lime trains for British Steel from Tunstead to Port Talbot. They were later coded CBA for TOPS purposes. Further builds of air-braked lime wagons

Nos 20041 and 20307 depart from Hindlow on 28 August 1986 with three wagonloads of lime for the glass industry, forming 7T82, the 1320 trip working to Peak Forest.

No 60071 *Ribblehead Viaduct* arrives at Tees Yard with 6N32 from Lackenby on 2 June 2006, comprising empty CBA lime wagons. It will couple up to the rake of HGAs from Redcar visible on the left of the photograph and the combined train will depart as 6M46 to Hardendale.

were either owned by or leased to the steel industry: they included two batches of PAB/PAA hoppers built by Standard Wagon in 1970 and 1972, and a batch of PAA (later PBA) hoppers built by BREL at Ashford in 1974/75. The Standard Wagon PAAs carried lime from the British Steel works at Hardendale to Lackenby, and the Ashford-built wagons – nicknamed 'white ladies' because of their persistent white bodyside stains – worked between Hardendale and Ravenscraig.

In 1990 Port Talbot switched its source of supply from Tunstead to Hardendale, still using the BR-owned CBA wagons but later supplemented by some privately owned bogie Polybulks. That flow continued until 2001, by which time all the CBAs

had been replaced by a pool of 16 JIA former grain hoppers. The Hardendale to Ravenscraig traffic ceased with the closure of Ravenscraig works, but the Scottish 'white ladies' were transferred to the Lackenby flow and subsequently purchased by EWS, at which point they were recoded from PBA to CBA. At the time of writing the Hardendale to Lackenby lime is conveyed on the same train that carries limestone from Hardendale to Redcar, the two portions being separated at Tees Yard.

The glass-making industry uses substantial quantities of lime. In the Speedlink era the kilns at Dowlow dispatched wagonloads of lime for glass-making to Mossend and Barnby Dun. Both these flows ceased in 1991, but the Mossend traffic resumed when Transrail launched its Enterprise network and is still operating twice weekly at the time of writing. Various types of covered hopper wagon have been used on the Mossend service, including two-axle PAA wagons in the 1980s and bogie JAA and JIA Polybulks in more recent years.

2.

Cement, bricks and blocks

In the late 1960s BR carried bulk cement on many parts of the network, mainly using purpose-built Presflo wagons that had been introduced in the 1950s. Each Presflo wagon could each carry between 20 and 22 tons of cement; they were discharged using compressed air and their bodies were reinforced with a grid of horizontal and vertical ribs to prevent distortion during discharge. Most Presflos were in railway ownership, but some belonged to Associated Portland Cement (APCM, later to become Blue Circle) and a few to Tunnel Cement. The BR-owned wagons were later coded CPV, and the privately owned vehicles PCV. In addition to regular flows to dedicated terminals, Presflos could turn up in station goods yards almost anywhere on the network, especially where there were major construction projects.

Alongside the Presflos, APCM operated a fleet of 285 Cemflo wagons, built between 1961 and 1965. The Cemflos differed from Presflos in having a cylindrical barrel to overcome the problem of cement sticking to internal corners, an aluminium body in order to minimise tare weight and maximise the payload, and simpler air-assisted discharge, which obviated the need for bodyside ribs. The Cemflos were used on various block flows, including the famous Cliffe to Uddingston working, which covered a distance of more than 450 miles.

The Cemflos soon became yesterday's technology as British Rail decided to switch from vacuum-braked to air-braked freight stock in the mid-1960s. At around the same time BR also decided to stop building specialised wagons of its own, forcing its customers to invest in their own fleets. APCM was quick to respond to these changes and introduced its first air-braked cement wagons in 1966. Two designs were tried out, one with a simple cylindrical barrel and the other with a barrel that sloped inwards towards the central

One of the last Class 50s to remain on the London Midland Region after the West Coast Main Line was electrified, No 50012 heads north near Ormside with a block train of Presflos from Tring to Gunnie on 18 June 1975. *Tom Heavyside*

discharge outlet. Both types were later coded PCA. Between 1966 and 1981 APCM/Blue Circle acquired more than 600 PCAs, mostly the 'depressed centre' type, and they could be seen operating out of all the company's rail-connected plants. APCM also ordered a small number of bogie cement wagons from 1969 onwards, each consisting of two 'depressed centre' tanks mounted on a bogied underframe. Coded PDA, they were a familiar sight on several routes, including Northfleet to Dunstable and Theale.

The older practice of carrying bagged cement in vans continued on a limited scale in the 1970s, using railway-owned vans as well as a fleet of nearly 100 PVV pallet vans owned by APCM. However, this traffic ceased in the early 1980s and the remaining PVVs were either stored or converted for other uses.

During the 1970s the demand for cement in Britain grew sharply as concrete became a more popular material for buildings and for road surfaces. BR benefited from this growth and gained a number of new long- and short-term contracts. In 1971 APCM opened its Northfleet plant, which ranked as the largest cement works in the world and was designed to rely on rail for inward deliveries of coal and gypsum as well as outgoing trainloads of cement. However, although more

No 47103 leaves Earles Sidings, Hope, with 6H76, the 1950 cement train to Northenden, on 28 August 1986. At that time vacuum-braked Presflos were still used on trains from Hope to Northenden and Melton.

Pilot loco No 08832 shunts PCA tanks at Birmingham Curzon Street on 30 July 1990. The tanks will form 6R63, the 1235 departure to Penyffordd.

Blue Circle Hope train plan, May 1972

Code	Dep	Days	From	To
6E13	0125	MX	Earles Sidings	Middlesbrough
6M45	0206	WFO	Earles Sidings	Beeston
6E58	0240	MX	Earles Sidings	Dewsbury
6M45	0300	MO	Earles Sidings	Beeston
6H34	0936	ThSX	Earles Sidings	Northenden
6M45	1442	SO	Earles Sidings	Beeston
6F39	1544	SX	Earles Sidings	Widnes
6E65	1735	SO	Earles Sidings	Dewsbury
6F52	2223	SX	Earles Sidings	Widnes

Blue Circle Eastgate train plan, October 1976

Code	Dep	Days	From	To
6S31	0630	TThO	Eastgate	Irvine
6K20	1354	EWD	Eastgate	Heaton
6K27	2230	MWO	Eastgate	Sunderland South Dock

Blue Circle Oxwellmains train plan, October 1976

Code	Dep	Days	From	To
6K30	0040	MX	Oxwellmains	Grangemouth
6K30	0155	MO	Oxwellmains	Grangemouth
6F14	0653	SX	Oxwellmains	Irvine
6L29	1055	SO	Oxwellmains	Dundee
6N53	1154	SO	Oxwellmains	Inverness
6A60	1223	SO	Oxwellmains	Aberdeen
6A01	1903	SX	Oxwellmains	Aberdeen
6N52	1945	SX	Oxwellmains	Inverness

No 25172 leaves Oxwellmains cement works with Cemflos on 17 June 1976. On the left is a rake of PVV cement vans. *Tom Heavyside*

than 70 cement terminals retained their rail connection in the mid-1970s, an increasing proportion of the tonnage was handled at a decreasing number of locations. Some of the smaller works, such as Chinnor and Fulbourne, dispatched their cement by road and retained their rail connection only to receive coal.

By the end of the 1970s all the major cement companies were using air-braked stock on at least some of their flows. The Government's Section 8 Grant scheme helped to fund some new wagons and terminal facilities; for example, in 1977 Ribblesdale Cement received a £500,000 grant to move cement from Clitheroe to Middlesbrough and Newcastle. Most of the wagons built in the 1970s and 1980s were two-axle PCAs of broadly similar design to those introduced by APCM in the late 1960s. However, Tunnel Cement opted for an unusual twin-cone design, coded PIA, for some of its traffic from Pitstone works near Tring.

The 1980s were a mixed decade for rail-borne cement traffic. A high-profile gain for the railway in 1982 was Ribblesdale's flow from Clitheroe to Gunnie (Coatbridge), routed via the West Coast Main Line and hauled by a pair of Class 37s throughout. For that traffic Ribblesdale acquired 36 PDA bogie tanks for finished cement, plus 16 PBA bogie covered hopper wagons for cement

Class 17 'Clayton' No D8568 saw two spells in industrial use after its withdrawal from BR in 1971 – first at Hemelite, Hemel Hempstead, then at Ribblesdale Cement, Clitheroe. It is pictured shunting PCA cement tanks at Clitheroe on 16 September 1981. *Tom Heavyside*

clinker, ie partly processed cement that has not yet been ground together with gypsum or anhydrite to give it suitable setting qualities. The cement clinker flow turned out to be short-lived, but the finished cement stayed on rail for a decade.

Downward pressures on rail-borne cement traffic included a rise in cheaper imports and the end of an industry-wide common pricing agreement in 1987, which made long-distance flows less cost-effective. The costs of using rail compared with road were also rising, especially low-volume wagonload traffic. By 1988 Blue Circle had stopped distributing cement by rail from Westbury and Plymstock and from its newly acquired Aberthaw plant, while forwardings from Swanscombe were reduced to a single intermittent flow to Aberdeen for the North Sea oil industry. Even Northfleet was no longer the busy rail freight centre that it had once been, with only one service to Theale remaining by the end of the decade.

The cement works at Penyffordd (Tunnel), Tring (Tunnel), Clitheroe (Ribblesdale) and Ketton (Ketton Cement) all came under the ownership of RTZ, joined later by Castle Cement. Rail forwardings from Penyffordd and Tring ceased in 1990, while traffic from Ketton was reduced to a single flow to London King's Cross. Meanwhile Rugby Cement withdrew completely from rail-borne cement distribution, its last timetabled service being a conditional path from Halling to Greenford that ended in 1991.

The reduction in traffic in the late 1980s enabled the withdrawal of the last vacuum-braked Presflos and Cemflos, latterly restricted to specific

Electro-diesels Nos 73137 *Royal Observer Corps* and 73123 stand in the Rugby Cement sidings at Halling before departing with PCA cement tanks for Scunthorpe on 6 July 1987.

trainload duties out of Hope and Oxwellmains. Many of the more modern air-braked wagons also became redundant; the Blue Circle bogie PDAs were an early target for withdrawal and many PCAs went into storage. A small number of the stored PCAs later found other uses, including fly ash from Longannet to Westbury and lime from Dowlow to Uskmouth.

The demise of BR's Speedlink wagonload network in 1991 made it more difficult for the cement companies to keep their small-scale flows on rail. Blue Circle, for example, had used Speedlink to distribute small quantities of sulphate-resistant cement from Eastgate to various receiving terminals. From summer 1991 a stand-alone network had to be set up for that traffic: it was conveyed by an existing company train from Eastgate to Tees Yard, a new company train from Tees Yard to Earles Sidings (Hope), then by existing company trains from Earles Sidings to

No 37172 arrives at Eastgate with 6E30, the 2218 empties from Grangemouth, on 24 May 1982.

Blue Circle sample programme, September 1992

Code	Dep	Days	From	To	
6F69	0135	WSO	Earles Sidings	Ditton for Widnes	
6E78	0237	WThSO	Earles Sidings	Dewsbury	
6E79	0847	WThO	Earles Sidings	Dewsbury	
6E94	0847	TFO	Earles Sidings	Kirton Lindsey	
6M90	1438	MThO	Earles Sidings	Beeston	
6H61	1812	MSX	Earles Sidings	Northenden	
6E73	2150	WO	Earles Sidings	Tees Yard	traffic to Carlisle
6N45	1304	SX	Eastgate	Tees Yard	
6N56	0430	WSX	Tees Yard	Newcastle	traffic from Eastgate to Widnes and Northenden
6N56	0641	WO	Tees Yard	Newcastle	
6N22	0715	SX	Tees Yard	Middlesbrough	
6S63	1558	MThO	Tees Yard	Millerhill	traffic from Eastgate to Scottish depots
6M26	1613	FO	Tees Yard	Bescot	
6M16	1626	WO	Tees Yard	Earles Sidings	
6D39	0720	MX	Oxwellmains	Mossend	traffic to Grangemouth and Aberdeen
6D38	1227	SX	Oxwellmains	Viewpark	also calls at Millerhill to detach traffic to Inverness
6D28	1637	SX	Oxwellmains	Viewpark	

CEMENT, BRICKS AND BLOCKS

depots such as Widnes, Northenden and Handsworth. In Scotland cement from Oxwellmains to Grangemouth and Inverness was conveyed by a Trainload Freight-sponsored 'bulklink' service. But that arrangement was fragile, as its viability depended on there being regular loads of oil and coal as well as cement.

As the railways prepared for privatisation, the Trainload Freight division of BR strengthened its efforts to weed out unprofitable freight flows and only the most robust trainload services survived. By 1993 all traffic from Clitheroe, now owned by Castle Cement, had ceased, as had the remaining business from Northfleet and Eastgate. The only cement flows remaining on rail at the end of 1993 were Ketton to King's Cross (Castle), Hope to Dewsbury, Northenden and Widnes (Blue Circle), and Oxwellmains to Uddingston and Aberdeen (Blue Circle). With no further investment taking place in rolling-stock or terminals, it seemed just a matter of time before rail-borne cement would be consigned to history.

Thankfully, the remaining cement flows survived the 1994 carve-up of Trainload Freight. The Castle Cement business from Ketton became a Class 58-hauled Mainline Freight operation, while the various Blue Circle flows from Hope and Oxwellmains passed to Transrail, generally using Class 60s. The traffic from Oxwellmains to Aberdeen did not warrant a full trainload; the loaded wagons used a shared Transrail/Railfreight Distribution service from Mossend to Aberdeen and the empties returned on a similarly shared train from Aberdeen to Millerhill. Transrail regained the flow from Hope to Beeston in 1995, although that revival did not last long.

The early years of EWS brought a more sustained revival of rail-borne cement. Ironically it was the closure of Plymstock cement works in 1999 that produced the first new flow: Blue Circle now needed to supply its customers in the South West from further afield and was able to justify a rail-served distribution terminal on the former china clay dries site at Moorswater. EWS introduced a twice-weekly train from Hope to Moorswater in July 1999, conveying bagged cement in IWB vans as well as bulk cement in PCA tanks. In Scotland, EWS started moving intermittent trainloads of cement from Oxwellmains to Ayr for export to Ireland. And in North West England, Blue Circle built a new cement distribution terminal next to the Manchester Ship Canal at Weaste, which would replace the two smaller railheads at Northenden and Weaste with the added potential of carrying traffic for export.

However, not all plans for expansion were fulfilled. Plans to re-open the 18-mile Caldon Low branch for Blue Circle cement as well as stone traffic came to nothing. In 2000 Blue Circle won a £2.9 million prize from the Strategic Rail Authority to launch an intermodal service, the money being used to fund 22 Babcock Mega 3 intermodal wagons and 22 road trailers. Trial runs with that equipment took place in 2003/04, mainly from Westbury to Southampton Millbrook, but the rail element of the operation was soon ditched and only the SRA-funded road trailers then remained in use.

The opening of Blue Circle's Weaste terminal in July 2000 marked the end of EWS's monopoly of bulk rail freight, as Blue Circle appointed Freightliner as its haulier for this flow and for the existing flows from Hope to Dewsbury. In 2002 Freightliner took over the rest of the Blue Circle cement flows, from Oxwellmains as well as Hope. At the same time Blue Circle, which was now part of the international Lafarge group, fulfilled its aim of sending more cement by rail: by 2004 new terminals were in operation at Carlisle Brunthill, Seaham and Theale, as well as a short-term railhead at Colnbrook for the building of Heathrow's new Terminal 5. The Carlisle and Seaham terminals each received traffic from both Hope and Oxwellmains, with the Hope-Carlisle train conveying bagged cement in vans.

The switch from EWS to Freightliner had one detrimental effect on rail freight in Scotland: it took away a large proportion of the traffic on EWS's Enterprise wagonload services to Aberdeen and Inverness and therefore placed other wagonload flows in jeopardy.

Some compensation for EWS for the loss of the

Cement traffic to Inverness ceased in the early 1990s but later resumed thanks to the Enterprise wagonload network. On 20 August 1998 PCA cement tanks form the entire load for 6H54, the 1312 Aberdeen to Inverness service, pictured at Elgin behind former Transrail locomotive No 37153.

The cement terminal at Dewsbury has survived various changes of wagon type, traction and operator. Freightliner Heavy Haul No 66559 pulls the last portion of its train out of the terminal on 7 April 2005, before departing with 6M89, the 0953 to Earles Sidings.

Blue Circle business came in November 2002, when Castle Cement signed a ten-year contract with EWS to continue its existing flow from Ketton to London. The destination for this flow would switch from King's Cross to St Pancras in 2003 as the King's Cross sidings were swallowed up by the Channel Tunnel Rail Link, a change that meant re-routeing the train via Leicester and the Midland Main Line instead of via Peterborough and the East Coast Main Line, even though the actual new terminal site was adjacent to the old one.

A further fillip for EWS in 2004 was a new seven-year contract with Buxton Lime Industries, the lime and cement division of Tarmac Building Products, to move cement from its new dry-process plant at Tunstead to three distribution terminals at Leeds, Walsall and Willesden. A £12 million Freight Facilities Grant contributed to the cost of 30 new 90-tonne-capacity bogie wagons as well as new terminal facilities. The wagons, coded JGA, were built by Arbel Fauvet of Douai, France, and were the first new bulk cement tanks to appear on Britain's railways since the late 1980s. At the time of writing several Class 60-hauled trains operate each week to Leeds and Walsall, with a weekly path to Willesden.

In the last few years various changes have taken

place with the Lafarge (Blue Circle) traffic. The flows of bagged cement in vans to Carlisle and Moorswater ended in late 2005 and the remaining bulk traffic to Moorswater ceased in August 2006. However, Moorswater was revived in late 2007 for what was expected to become a weekly train of bulk cement from Westbury.

Meanwhile Lafarge announced a revamp of its rail operations at Hope early in 2006, with the aim of increasing its rail output from 750,000 tonnes to more than 1 million tonnes a year. The company obtained planning permission for new loading facilities at Hope and placed an order for 48 bogie cement wagons, to be manufactured by Feldbinder and leased to Lafarge by VTG Rail. Lafarge also announced the opening of a new terminal at West Thurrock on the Thames estuary, with the potential to handle imported cement as well as domestic traffic from Hope.

Plasmor adopted Biggleswade goods yard as one of its main distribution railheads for construction blocks manufactured at Heck. No 31141 shunts OBA wagons at Biggleswade after arriving with 6B30, the 0754 feeder service from Peterborough.

A long-awaited piece of good news in 2007 was Castle Cement's decision to re-start the rail-borne movement of cement from Clitheroe to Scotland after a gap of 15 years. Fortunately Castle had retained the main-line connection and sidings at Clitheroe for other traffic, mainly inward coal together with occasional deliveries of iron oxide. An initial batch of 15 JPA bogie cement tanks was delivered in 2008, of similar design to those supplied to Lafarge.

●

Bricks and blocks have been carried by rail on various routes in the last 40 years. London Brick introduced a containerised operation from Stewartby to London, Manchester and Liverpool in the early 1970s, using Freightliner wagons and Freightliner terminals at King's Cross, Trafford Park and Garston. At its height this operation handled a total of 3.2 million bricks a week, but was lost to road haulage in the early 1980s.

A private siding at Heck, north of Doncaster, was provided for Plasmor in 1988, enabling the company to move wagonloads of breeze blocks by

The TransManche Link terminal at Shakespeare Cliff is pictured on 21 August 1989, with No 09024 shunting two PXA and two POA wagons carrying concrete tunnel segments from Grain.

rail to destinations in the South East. The traffic switched to trainload operation in 1991, with a daily service to Biggleswade and/or Bow and a twice-weekly connection to Wymondham. The traffic to Biggleswade and Bow lasted into the 21st century, using a mixture of railway-owned OAA open wagons and Plasmor's own PNA conversions. EWS signed a ten-year contract with Plasmor for this business in 2003. A similar flow has operated from Merehead to Acton for many years, comprising Forticrete building blocks manufactured near Merehead Quarry for distribution in the London area. At the time of writing a raft of OAA wagons carrying the Forticrete blocks is added to one of the daily 'jumbo trains' from Merehead to Acton. Many of the wagons have been fitted with mesh sides instead of the original wooden planking. The original OAA design was introduced in 1971 as the 'Open AB', intended for general merchandise traffic on BR's new air-braked services.

3.

Waste

The rail freight revolution of the 1960s and 1970s brought, among other things, the demise of the last old-style rubbish trains – slow, smelly, loose-coupled goods trains carrying some of London's refuse to an unsophisticated dump on the rump of the former Welwyn to Luton line. But it wasn't long before rail-borne refuse traffic started up again, in a very different form. In 1977 the Greater London Council opened its rail-served waste transfer station at Brentford, where household waste from several boroughs in West London could be compacted and loaded into totally enclosed 20-foot containers, ready for trainload movement on Freightliner-type flat wagons to Appleford landfill site near Didcot.

Two further schemes in the London area were

The huge landfill site at Calvert ensured the survival of a section of the former Great Central main line between Aylesbury and Claydon. No 47599 pulls forward at Calvert while its train is loaded on 9 July 1986, before forming 4V04, the 1230 departure to Bath.

established in the late 1970s and early 1980s. One connected Hendon (Cricklewood in railway terms) transfer station with Stewartby (Forders Sidings) landfill site, on the Bedford to Bletchley line. The other ran from Hillingdon (Northolt) to Calvert, north of Aylesbury.

Both Stewartby and Calvert were former London Brick sites where many decades of clay extraction had produced some very large holes in the ground. At Stewartby the waste transfer sidings were formerly used to load bricks for 'Fletliner' trains to London, Manchester and Liverpool. At Calvert one long loop line and siding adjacent to the former Great Central main line – closed to passengers since the 1960s – was adapted to its new waste-handling role.

The contract for the Cricklewood to Stewartby flow was awarded to Freightliner Heavy Haul in late 2001, which replaced the twice-daily service with a single, longer train. With the holes in the ground at Stewartby filling up rapidly, the destination for the Cricklewood traffic switched to Calvert in 2005. By

The Dean Lane to Appley Bridge refuse train was diverted to run round at Southport after the loop at Burscough was taken out of use. No 60016 *Langdale Pikes* departs from the seaside terminus with 6F77, the 1245 from Dean Lane to Appley Bridge, on 9 July 1993.

this time Freightliner Heavy Haul was also operating a daily train of refuse from Dagenham to Calvert. For the traffic from Cricklewood and Dagenham Freightliner Heavy Haul provided a fleet of FRA/FEA wagons. EWS retained the Northolt to Calvert and Brentford to Appleford flows.

Greater Manchester Council began dispatching household waste by rail in 1981 and eventually opened four transfer stations at Northenden, Bredbury, Pendleton and Dean Lane. The refuse was originally offloaded at a former quarry landfill site at Appley Bridge, between Wigan and Southport. It was temporarily diverted to Wakefield in 1987 because of a delay in extending the planning permission at Appley Bridge, but returned to Appley Bridge in the following year.

When the Appley Bridge site became full in 1993, the Manchester refuse trains were diverted to a landfill site in former ironstone workings at Roxby, near Scunthorpe. This change increased the length of the rail haul from 25-30 miles to 80-90 miles. The traffic was suspended in 1995 but restarted in 1997, with a daily schedule of one train from Northenden, one from Bredbury and a combined train from Pendleton and Dean Lane. In 2005 the Greater Manchester Waste Disposal Authority renewed its contract with EWS for a further seven years, against stiff competition from other rail and road operators.

Avon County Council launched a rail-based refuse disposal scheme in 1986. It built two new transfer stations – Bristol Barrow Road and Bath Midland Road – from scratch, and adapted a third – Westerleigh – for rail access. A single daily train conveyed portions from all three transfer stations to Calvert, using customer-owned PFA (later KFA) wagons. In 2001 the contract for this traffic switched from EWS to Freightliner Heavy Haul, but the Westerleigh terminal was closed following the opening of an incineration plant in the north Bristol area and the train therefore only served Bath and Bristol. The whole operation was expected to cease in 2008.

Edinburgh was the next municipal waste authority after Avon to opt for a rail-based waste disposal scheme. The City of Edinburgh invested in a purpose-built transfer station at Powderhall on the former Granton branch and acquired its own fleet of 13 PFA (later KFA) bogie wagons. The service was inaugurated in 1989 and ran initially to Kaimes, on the line to Glasgow via Shotts. In 1997 Kaimes reached its capacity and trains were diverted to the huge landfill site at Dunbar, beside Oxwellmains cement works.

A number of other waste disposal authorities have evaluated 'waste by rail' schemes. Westminster City Council considered a rail-based scheme in 1988/89, using a proposed railhead either at White City or in Westminster. However, the scheme was abandoned, partly because of changes in the legislation under which local authorities operate and partly because of rival claims on the land at both proposed railhead sites. Possible schemes from Devon, Hampshire and Kent failed to come to fruition; often the start-up costs of rail are simply too high and the number of suitably high-volume flows to landfill sites is declining as councils promote local recycling and incineration instead.

●

No 47004 runs round its train of empty refuse containers at Powderhall on 31 August 1990. At that time the refuse from Powderhall was destined for Kaimes.

No 37359 passes Croxton lime works with 6D85, the 0723 Grimsby to Roxby gypsum waste train, on 23 October 1993. This traffic was one of the last flows gained by Railfreight Distribution, shortly before BR was privatised.

One of several short-term waste flows won by BR involved removing toxic waste from a former factory site at Barking to the former London Brick claypits at Stewartby (Forders Sidings). No 47367 pulls away from Forders Sidings with the 6Z59 empties to Barking on 17 July 1989.

Alongside household refuse, the railway has carried various flows of industrial waste, often in connection with the redevelopment of 'brownfield' sites. From 1993 until December 2001 a flow of containerised red gypsum waste ran from the Tioxide works at Grimsby to Roxby. A pool of 12 Tiphook bogie wagons was allocated to this traffic, with each wagon conveying three 20-foot containers.

Short-term flows of contaminated soil and hardcore have included Willesden to Stewartby in 1989-90, Chatham to Stewartby in 1990-91, Norwich to Calvert in 1997, Hastings to Allington in 1998-99, Thames Haven to Calvert in 2001-02, and King's Cross to Calvert in 2002-04. Calvert also received a number of trainloads of containerised ash from burned foot-and-mouth carcasses from Teesside and South Wales in 2001. The combination of long- and short-term flows to Calvert required the provision of an additional discharge siding at the landfill site in 2002, supported by a £1.5 million grant from the Strategic Rail Authority.

An ambitious project that failed to live up to expectations was Bow Midland Waste Recycling. Built during 2001 on a strategic 4½-acre site west of Stratford at a cost of some £4 million, including a £1.7 million Freight Facilities Grant, it comprised a separation and screening facility for construction and demolition waste, plus two rail sidings and a run-round loop to enable the non-recyclable residue to be loaded into rail-borne containers. The output from Bow Midland was divided into three types: non-recyclable sub-soil, non-recyclable hardcore, and the non-recyclable residue from all the materials that had been separated and screened, eg plastics and Rockwool. The three types were loaded into separate containers for movement in a single trainload to the landfill site, initially Stewartby but later Calvert. Trains ran intermittently during 2002 but the project was then abandoned and the wagons and containers were redeployed elsewhere. However, the sidings at Bow saw further use in late 2007 when EWS began moving spoil to Calvert in connection with redevelopment work for the London Olympics.

4.

Minerals

China clay

Synonymous with Cornish rail freight in the 1970s and 1980s were the distinctive 'clay hoods' for carrying bulk china clay to the harbour at Fowey. The same basic wagon design had been in use since the late 19th century – two-axle wooden-bodied vehicles with a carrying capacity between 10 and 12½ tons. They were open-topped to facilitate

The former goods shed and mechanical signalling lend a period feel to this view of No 37142 arriving at Lostwithiel with 'clay hoods' for Fowey on 2 August 1982. Today there is no trace of the goods shed or the up-side sidings, but the bracket semaphore signal remains.

loading from above and had side and/or end doors for discharge. The last generation comprised a fleet of 875 vehicles built to a standard British Railways design between 1954 and 1960. For TOPS purposes they were coded UCV, later altered to OOV.

Originally the clay wagons were tarpaulined to keep the clay free from moisture during transit. However, the tarpaulins were easily torn or damaged and tended to gather water in the corners. In 1974/75, therefore, BR fitted all wagons in use on the Fowey circuit with single raised ridge bars and blue plastic sheets, giving them a tent-like appearance when in normal operation – hence the name 'clay hoods'. As well

as preventing the formation of water pockets, the ridge bars ensured that the sheeting did not stick to the load.

In the early 1980s the 'clay hoods' operated out of 11 English China Clays dries in Cornwall and Devon. One of the main sources of traffic was the freight-only Parkandillack branch, with loading points at Parkandillack, Treviscoe, Kernick and Drinnick Mill. Where the Parkandillack branch joins the main line there were loading points at Crugwallins and Burngullow. Another busy loading point was Goonbarrow, also known as Rocks, on the Newquay branch. Further east, the 'clay hoods' carried china clay from Wenford Bridge, Moorswater and Marsh Mills as well as ball clay from Heathfield.

Operations to and from Wenford Bridge were hampered by the need for all trains to reverse direction three times, at Boscarne Junction, Bodmin General and Bodmin Road. Furthermore main-line traction was prohibited beyond Boscarne Junction and a Class 08 had to be used on the final stretch to Wenford Bridge. It therefore came as little surprise when the Wenford Bridge branch closed in 1983.

Trainloads of 'clay hoods' produced a wide variety of diesel traction. In the late 1960s they were hauled by Western Region hydraulics, including the short-lived Class 22s. From the early 1970s until 1980 a small fleet of Class 25s took over the bulk of Cornish china clay traffic. The first Class 37s arrived in 1978, followed by a

dedicated pool of refurbished Class 37/5s in 1986.

The fleet of 'clay hoods' declined to approximately 500 vehicles by the mid-1980s and by this time it was clear that a more modern replacement would soon be necessary. Apart from the fact that some were more than 30 years old, the 'clay hoods' had very limited capacity, were vacuum-braked and were restricted to 45mph on the main line.

Following trials with open coal hoppers, and with the promise of a 15-year contract with English China Clays, BR ordered 124 air-braked china clay wagons in 1987. Coded CDA, the new wagons had a carrying capacity of 32 tonnes and were basically a hooded version of the highly successful HAA 'merry-go-round' coal hopper. New bottom-door discharge facilities were installed at Fowey and the new wagons entered revenue-earning service on 26 January 1988.

The tonnages handled at Fowey remained healthy in the 1990s, with operations coming under the control of Transrail, then EWS. The wagon fleet was boosted by 15 additional CDAs converted from coal hoppers, and in 1998 the throughput at Fowey reached its highest ever total of 847,000 tonnes. However, the number of loading terminals declined: the dries at Moorswater closed in 1997, pending conversion to a cement distribution terminal, and ball clay traffic from Heathfield finished around the same time.

English China Clays became part of the

No 37669 shunts Tiger covered hoppers and European-registered vans at Kernick clay dries on the Parkandillack branch on 16 February 1988. Most of the traffic would travel forward from St Blazey using the Speedlink network.

The unloading facility for CDA hopper wagons at Came Point, Fowey, is pictured on 16 February 1988, shortly after its commissioning.

international Imerys group in 1999. Efforts were made to increase efficiency by running fewer, heavier trains, with the standard load rising from 16 to 24 wagons in 2002. Imerys signed a new five-year contract with EWS in 2007, with the promise of a further increase in train lengths; however, the overall tonnages moved from Cornwall were expected to decline in favour of increased imports from Brazil.

In addition to the Fowey traffic, BR transported clay from Cornwall and Devon to numerous UK destinations and via train ferry to mainland Europe. In the 1970s traffic to the Potteries in Staffordshire warranted a block train, comprising wooden-bodied OWV open wagons that had been

fitted with roller bearings and zinc floors to prevent corrosion. In 1982 a Section 8 Grant kept this flow on rail with a new receiving terminal at Cliffe Vale and a new 35-strong fleet of air-braked 56-tonne-capacity covered hopper wagons, leased to English China Clays by Tiger Rail. Coded PBA (later JAA), they had a high-quality internal finish to prevent contamination between successive loads of different grades of clay.

Long before the Tiger Rail initiative, the first Cornish china clay flow to go over to air-braked block train operation had been slurry from Burngullow to Bowaters at Sittingbourne. This flow used a fleet of 20 purpose-built TTA tank wagons introduced from 1966 – the first year in

No 73134 prepares to depart from Strood goods yard with empty OWV china clay wagons forming the 1255 service to Hoo Junction on 10 June 1981. On the right is the industrial shunter *Telemon*, since preserved and based at Oswestry at the time of writing.

The discharge terminal at Cliffe Vale, Stoke, is pictured on 4 July 1986, with No 47200 in charge of a neat rake of Tiger bogie hopper wagons. The empties will depart as 6V70, the 1402 Cliffe Vale to Exeter.

which most new freight stock in Britain was air-braked rather than vacuum-braked.

Other china clay flows used mainly wagonload services, gradually transferring to air-braked Speedlink operation in the late 1970s and early 1980s. The shift to Speedlink brought a wide variety of wagon types, making for some interesting train formations for the lineside observer. Bagged clay to more than 20 destinations such as Duxford, Selby and Worcester was carried in VAA, VDA and VGA vans; bagged clay to mainland Europe used a mixture of two-axle and bogie ferry vans; bulk powdered clay to Mossend used Tiger Rail PBAs; bulk powdered clay to Auchmuty used two-axle PAA covered hopper wagons; bulk powdered clay to Corpach used unique PRA covered hopper wagons; bulk powdered clay to Biberist in Switzerland used PIB Polybulk wagons; and slurry to Sittingbourne, Warrington, Mossend, Aberdeen and Port Elphinstone used a mixture of TTA, TUA, TCA, TDA and TIA tank wagons.

The Biberist traffic was a semi-trainload operation, with two 11- or 12-wagon trains running from Plymouth (Tavistock Junction) Yard to Dover on successive days and joining to form a single 23-wagon train on the European mainland. For a time the Polybulks on this service were backloaded with imported grain to Pinhoe, near Exeter.

The loading points used for non-shipment traffic included most of the locations that served

Fowey, together with further terminals at Par Harbour, Pontsmill, Carbis Wharf and Newton Abbot. The Carbis Wharf operation was a remarkable survival in the diesel era: it was a dead-end siding with accommodation for one wagon and no run-round loop. It forwarded its last traffic in August 1989.

The opening of the Caledonian Paper mill at Irvine produced a new trainload china clay flow from Burngullow in March 1989. Covering a journey of some 550 miles, this was the longest-distance trainload freight service on BR. It used a purpose-built fleet of TIA 'silver bullet' bogie tank wagons, hauled throughout by a pair of Class 37 locomotives. Initially the service ran once a week, increasing later to two or three weekly trainloads.

The run-down and closure of Speedlink brought the loss of many wagonload china clay flows, while others were retained thanks to semi-trainload services sponsored initially by Tiger Rail and later by Railfreight Distribution. Transrail incorporated some china clay traffic into its Enterprise wagonload network, which was adopted and developed by EWS in 1996. However, by this time some of the smaller loading points such as Pontsmill and Newton Abbot had closed, as had some of the destinations, including Warrington, Auchmuty and Port Elphinstone. EWS continued to operate trainloads of china clay to mainland Europe, now destined for Sezzadio in Italy instead of Biberist.

Rolling-stock developments included the

Above Nos 37674 and 37669 pass Auchinleck with the empty 'silver bullets' from Irvine to Burngullow on 16 July 1992. This train brought Laira-based Class 37s to Scotland on a regular basis – quite a contrast with their local china clay duties in Cornwall.

Right Cornish china clay came under the control of Railfreight Distribution (RfD) even though the Fowey traffic operated in full trainloads. RfD-liveried locomotive No 37673 approaches St Blazey with CDAs from Goonbarrow to Lostwithiel on 16 February 1988.

conversion of a dozen ex-Tiger Rail JAAs to internationally registered JIAs in 1994, the introduction of 26 Imerys-branded JIA covered hoppers to replace life-expired ex-Tiger Rail stock in 2000 and the introduction of 30 TEA tanks to replace the original 'silver bullets' to Irvine in 2003. The surviving two-axle hoppers and tanks that carried clay were gradually withdrawn from service.

EWS made a brief attempt to capture new traffic in 1997 by hauling containerised clay from Cornwall to Southampton for export to the Far East. However, this experiment was not repeated.

Meanwhile volumes on the regular Sezzadio flow waned and in 2005 EWS switched the traffic to wagonload operation.

As for domestic traffic, the only destinations served from Cornwall by 2005 were Cliffe Vale, Irvine and Mossend. EWS introduced a new train plan in 2006 to make better use of resources, combining the Cliffe Vale and Irvine flows into a single twice-weekly train between Cornwall and the West Midlands. However, the Burngullow to Irvine train was replaced in January 2008 by a weekly service carrying Brazilian clay from Antwerp.

Industrial sand

The glass-making industry consumes large quantities of sand and has made extensive use of rail during the last 40 years. Until the 1980s the sand was carried in railway-owned wagons of various types, including MTV open box wagons, HKV open hoppers and CHO/P/V covered hopper wagons. BR operated regular flows from Oakamoor in Staffordshire to Worksop, St Helens and Wigan, and from Middleton Towers in Norfolk to various glassworks in South Yorkshire including Cudworth, Monk Bretton and Barnby Dun.

The traffic from Middleton Towers went over to air-braked operation following the introduction of 60 38-tonne PAA covered hopper wagons in 1981/82. These wagons had reinforced bodies and were suitable for carrying both dry and wet sand. In 1986 some of the PAAs replaced the remaining vacuum-braked stock on traffic from Oakamoor; however, only the flow to St Helens survived this change, with Wigan switching to road deliveries and Worksop being served from Middleton Towers. The Oakamoor to St Helens traffic then ceased in August 1988, leaving no further freight use for the 7½-mile branch from Leek Brook Junction to Oakamoor.

Alongside the company trains from Oakamoor and Middleton Towers, BR carried wagonloads of industrial sand from Holmethorpe near Redhill to the Crosfields plant at Warrington. Six PAA wagons had their roofs removed and were recoded

PGA for this flow in the 1980s. However, the Holmethorpe traffic ceased before the demise of Speedlink.

In the 1990s the Middleton Towers sand was allocated to Trainload Construction, then to Mainline Freight in the pre-privatisation carve-up. In 1996 a daily departure operated from Middleton Towers, serving either Monk Bretton or Worksop and Barnby Dun. Under EWS management the flows to Worksop and Barnby Dun continued without interruption, but the Monk Bretton traffic was suspended from July 1997 until 1999, casting doubt over the future of the freight-only branch from Crofton to Monk Bretton – formerly part of the Midland main line between Sheffield and Leeds. In 2003 EWS renewed its contract with WBB Minerals to move 147,000 tonnes of sand annually to Monk Bretton, 100,000 tonnes to Barnby Dun and 15,000 tonnes to Worksop.

In 2004 EWS signed a further contract to deliver 130,000 tonnes of sand a year from Middleton Towers to the new Guardian glassworks at Goole. For this traffic and for its existing flows WBB Minerals refurbished the 60 PAA wagons introduced in the early 1980s and acquired 12 additional wagons that had previously been used by Steetley to carry lime.

In late 2006 EWS gained a short-term opportunity to move sand from Middleton Towers to a glassworks in South West Scotland. The traffic was unloaded initially at Mossend, and later

Pilkington's at St Helens received sand by rail until the 1980s. No 47230 passes Ravenhead Junction box with 8F21, the 1512 departure from Oakamoor, on 30 August 1985. The train at that time conveyed sand for Wigan as well as St Helens.

Above Just after the introduction of air-braked PAA wagons on sand traffic from Oakamoor, Nos 20188 and 20121 pull away from the loading point with 9L37, the 1535 departure to Longport, on 27 August 1986. The wagons would go forward to St Helens the following day.

Right The new Guardian glassworks at Goole provided EWS with additional sand traffic from Middleton Towers. No 66180 draws forward at Goole with refurbished PAA wagons on 24 May 2007 before departing with 6H93, the 1704 empties to Peterborough.

at Ayr. It used HGA open hopper wagons, later switching to newly built HOA vehicles before finishing in May 2007.

●

A little-known and highly localised freight working was the movement of a special grade of imported sand, called ilmenite, from Immingham Docks to the Tioxide factory at Grimsby. Ilmenite is used in the production of titanium dioxide, a high-quality white paint pigment. The Tioxide flow operated intermittently until the 1990s depending on the arrival of ships at Immingham; in later years it used a fleet of unfitted PSO mineral wagons built on the underframes of redundant tank wagons in the 1970s.

Gypsum

In the 1960s and 1970s naturally occurring gypsum was transported by rail on a number of routes, mostly destined for the cement industry. One of the main forwarding points was the British Gypsum mine at East Leake (Hotchley Hill), located on the former Great Central main line between Loughborough and Nottingham, which continued to forward gypsum in vacuum-braked wagons until the early 1980s. In the South of England, the gypsum flow from Robertsbridge (Mountfield) to Northfleet became an air-braked trainload operation in 1970, using PGA hopper wagons similar in design to BR 'merry-go-round' coal hoppers. This traffic was the last rail-borne flow of naturally occurring gypsum and lasted until the early 1990s.

Anhydrite, a mineral similar to gypsum that is used in the manufacture of sulphuric acid and ammonium compounds for fertilisers, was transported by rail for many years from Long Meg mine, between Appleby and Carlisle, to Widnes. The trainloads of purpose-built anhydrite hopper wagons, later coded UYV, were a well-known feature of Settle & Carlisle line operations in the steam era and continued with diesel haulage into the 1970s.

Not long after the last rail-borne flow of naturally occurring gypsum ended, BR won a ten-year contract to move trainloads of desulphogypsum produced by the new flue gas desulphurisation plant at Drax power station. The desulphogypsum could be used to manufacture plasterboard in much the same way as the naturally occurring gypsum, but brought a significant cost saving because it was essentially a waste by-product rather than a mineral that needed to be mined.

The first destination for the rail-borne desulphogypsum was the British Gypsum plant at Kirkby Thore. This was the flow that brought revenue-earning freight traffic back to the central section of the Settle & Carlisle line in 1993 after a gap of ten years. BR also ran trainloads of desulphogypsum from Drax to Mountfield, bringing freight traffic back to the Hastings line.

The desulphogypsum was carried in 20-foot containers mounted on various types of intermodal wagon, including 24 KFA wagons built by Rautaruukki in 1994. They were later supplemented by former Cawoods two-axle PFA wagons and by EWS-owned FCA and FBA wagons. British Gypsum opted for containers because the desulphogypsum was too sticky to discharge reliably from hopper wagons and the use of tippler wagons would have required expensive handling equipment at the discharge terminals.

The desulphogypsum contract won by BR passed to Loadhaul, then to EWS. In 1998 two major developments took place. One was the re-opening of the 5¼-mile branch line from Loughborough to the British Gypsum plant at East Leake, which then became another destination for desulphogypsum from Drax. Railtrack later sold the East Leake branch to the Great Central Railway (Nottingham), which would use it for passenger services at weekends.

The other development of 1998 was the start-up of imported gypsum traffic from Southampton Docks to Mountfield, replacing some of the tonnage railed from Drax. EWS also seized short-term opportunities to move imported gypsum from Workington, Hunterston and Hartlepool to Kirkby Thore.

The EWS monopoly of desulphogypsum trains was broken in 2002 when British Gypsum signed a contract with GB Railfreight for a proportion of its tonnage. The first GB Railfreight-hauled gypsum trains carried imported product from Hull Docks to Kirkby Thore, but in 2003 the company took over the existing flow from Southampton to Mountfield and gained new-to-rail traffic from West Burton power station to Kirkby Thore. GB Railfreight later added Cottam power station and East Leake to its network, with trains running between different terminals as required. GB Railfreight allocated some of its own FEA wagons to the gypsum traffic, as well as hiring IFA wagons from the Ahaus Alstätter Eisenbahn.

At the time of writing Kirkby Thore receives up to three desulphogypsum trains a day, mainly EWS-hauled from Drax, while East Leake receives a daily GB Railfreight-hauled train from West Burton or Cottam, and Mountfield receives a daily GB Railfreight-hauled train from Southampton. EWS also started regular movements of desulphogypsum from Drax to Gascoigne Wood in 2008, for onward delivery by road to the British Gypsum works at Sherburn.

MINERALS

Above The gypsum train from Mountfield to Northfleet was the last freight service to require the use of narrow-bodied Class 33/2 locomotives. No 33208 passes Stonegate with the loaded hoppers on 19 April 1984.

Below No 66219 passes the long-disused platforms of Rushcliffe Halt as it sets out with empty gypsum containers forming 6E76, the 1203 East Leake to Milford, on 26 July 2001. Rushcliffe Halt has since been restored to weekend passenger use by the Great Central Railway (Nottingham) Limited.

Potash and rock salt

Cleveland Potash operates the UK's only potash mine at Boulby, nestling above the cliffs of the North Sea coast and in the shadow of the North Yorkshire Moors. It opened in 1973 and today produces more than a million tonnes of potash a year, as well as more than half a million tonnes of rock salt. The potash is a raw material for the fertiliser, glass, chemical and pharmaceutical industries, while the salt is used for road maintenance, sugar beet processing and as an ingredient in animal feeds.

Rail access to Boulby mine was provided by re-opening a 5-mile stretch of the Skinningrove to Whitby line, which had closed as a through route in 1958. The re-opening took place in April 1974, after which BR ran an intensive freight service carrying potash from Boulby to Tees Dock for export and to Middlesbrough Goods for local distribution. For a time BR also carried some of the potash from Boulby to Severnside and Ely.

From the early 1980s the potash traffic was joined by increasing volumes of salt from Boulby to Middlesbrough Goods, where it was stockpiled for distribution by road to local authorities and county councils throughout the country. Eventually the combination of potash and salt traffic amounted to up to a dozen trains a day, covered by three locomotive diagrams.

Many different wagon types have appeared on the Boulby traffic. For many years the salt was carried in open wagons and containers, while the potash for Tees Dock and Middlesbrough initially used a fleet of 34 bogie covered hoppers built by Charles Roberts, later joined by a smaller fleet of two-axle PAA covered hoppers originally built by Procor for aggregate traffic. The Severnside flow used covered containers mounted on various types of flat wagon. For a short period some railway-owned CBA hoppers found their way on to the Boulby circuit, but corrosion was a problem and they were soon withdrawn.

In the 1990s the Boulby traffic followed the national trend towards bogie wagons. W. H. Davis supplied seven JGA bogie hoppers for potash in 1991, still in use at the time of writing and identifiable by their angular rather than curved outline. A Freight Facilities Grant supported the provision of 31 Arbel Fauvet-built JGA hoppers for salt traffic in 1998, and a larger fleet of similar-looking JIA hoppers was introduced for potash in 2002.

The Boulby trains hung on to Class 56 haulage longer than most other flows on Teesside, with Classes 60 and 66 finally taking over in 2003. When the contract came up for renewal in 2007, Cleveland Potash awarded it to Freightliner Heavy Haul, giving that company its biggest toehold so far in the Teesside freight market. Operations continued much as before, except that Tees Yard was no longer used as a run-round location.

No 60007 *Robert Adam* approaches Skinningrove on 23 February 1995 with a mixed consist of rock salt and potash forming 6P23, the 1355 departure from Boulby.

MINERALS

Another forwarding point for rock salt was Over & Wharton in Cheshire. For many years BR ran trainloads of salt in OWV open wagons to various destinations in Scotland. In later years HEA hopper wagons were used, but the traffic declined and the Over & Wharton branch closed in 1991.

However, in 2003 Salt Union received a Freight Facilities Grant totalling £640,000 from Scottish Executive and the Strategic Rail Authority to move 40,000 tonnes of salt each year from Winsford to Grangemouth, using an EWS intermodal service from Trafford Park.

Right **Just after running round its train at Grangetown, No 66602 takes the single-track branch to Tees Dock with the 6F32 potash train from Boulby on 1 June 2007.**

Below **No 40109 passes the then closed Dent station with 6S52 from Winsford on 8 September 1980, carrying rock salt in OWV wagons. This service operated to Cadder, Millerhill or Tyne Yard as required.**

Fly ash

Fly ash, also known as pulverised fuel ash (PFA), is the finely divided mineral residue resulting from the combustion of coal in electricity generating plants. It is incombustible and has limited potential for commercial use, mainly as an ingredient in cement manufacturing and as an aggregate for road-building and other construction projects.

The building of a new generation of coal-fired plants in the UK in the 1960s led to a huge increase in the amount of fly ash produced – West Burton power station alone produced between 1 and 1½ million tonnes of ash annually. Only a small proportion of the ash could be sold for further use and the Central Electricity Generating Board (CEGB) therefore had to find a suitable place and method for dumping much of it.

After looking at various options the CEGB decided to dispose of the ash by filling in the London Brick Company's vast claypits at Fletton,

Lincoln Cathedral dominates the skyline as No 47365 takes the Lincoln avoiding line with 6D65, the 0806 Peterborough to West Burton fly ash empties, on 16 April 1983. The Lincoln avoiding line closed in November of that year.

near Peterborough. The pits had the capacity to take at least 30 million tonnes of ash. A rail operation was devised that mirrored the 'merry-go-round' system for coal: permanently coupled block trains of ash would be loaded at a continuous loop at West Burton and discharged at another continuous loop at Fletton. Because the ash had a tendency to compact during transit, BR built a fleet of reinforced wagons with pressurised discharge similar to the cement Presflo design. Those used on the West Burton to Fletton flow were air-braked and later coded CSA for TOPS purposes.

Regular trains of up to 48 CSA wagons began running from West Burton to Fletton in 1965. A similar service was introduced from Ratcliffe power station. Both West Burton and Ratcliffe continued to send out ash by rail throughout the 1980s. However, in 1984 some of the West Burton traffic was diverted to a plant on the site of Little Barford power station, between St Neots and Sandy, where the ash was processed for use by the then fast-growing construction industry. The 1989 timetable shows up to six trains a week from Ratcliffe to Fletton, two trains a week from West Burton to Fletton, and up to ten trains a week from West Burton to Little Barford.

Above No 37045 leaves Hams Hall with an empty train of CSV fly ash wagons for Drakelow power station on 7 January 1984. The land at Hams Hall is now occupied by a freight village and intermodal terminal.

Below New sidings were provided at Oakleigh, beside the Winnington plant of Brunner Mond, to handle fly ash for the Northwich stabilisation scheme. No 66078 prepares to depart from Oakleigh with 6Z56, the 1300 empties to Selby, on 5 April 2005. On the adjacent track are some of the CTA tanks that were intended to carry brine from Oakleigh to Middlewich; very little of that traffic ever ran.

The traffic to Fletton ceased in 1991, releasing the site for redevelopment. The Little Barford flow declined as the construction industry plunged into recession and the last train operated in 1994, making the remaining CSA wagons redundant.

Other flows of fly ash included regular trainload traffic from Drakelow to the former power station site at Hams Hall, which used vacuum-braked CSV wagons and ran until the mid-1980s, and several short-term flows for specific construction projects. In 1970, for example, trains operated from Aberthaw to Puxton in Somerset for the M4/M5 motorway construction, and in 1983 from Fiddlers Ferry to North Wales for the building of the A55 expressway. From 1997 until 2002 EWS used its Enterprise network to carry fly ash in PCA wagons from Longannet to Westbury cement works.

A major opportunity to carry ash by rail came about in 2002, when Vale Royal Borough Council received a £28 million grant to fill long-abandoned salt mines under the town of Northwich in order to protect buildings from subsidence and allow future development. The scheme involved filling almost 800,000 cubic metres of underground cavities, which had previously been filled with brine, with a solid material made up of 97% fly ash and 3% cement.

The fly ash was delivered to a temporary terminal beside the Brunner Mond works at Winnington (Oakleigh). It came mainly from Drax, using two 16-vehicle rakes of MBA bogie box wagons. The first train ran in January 2005 and traffic gradually built up to reach two trains each weekday with a single train on Saturday morning. The Drax flow was supplemented by a small number of EWS-hauled trains from Uskmouth and Freightliner-hauled trains from Ratcliffe. The last delivery of ash to Oakleigh took place in August 2007, after which the MBA wagons were redeployed on limestone traffic from the Peak District.

The construction of Heathrow Airport's Terminal 5 was another project requiring trainload deliveries of fly ash, alongside other construction materials such as cement, stone and steel. In 2003 EWS won a five-year contract to move ash from West Burton to Colnbrook, using bright orange Rugby tanktainers mounted on FCA intermodal wagons.

Iron ore

In the late 1960s many of the UK's blast furnaces were still fed with local ironstone or haematite. Rail was the dominant transport mode, and the ore was carried either in tippler wagons – flat-bottomed vehicles that were tipped upside down to discharge their load – or in hopper wagons. Some flows operated entirely over BSC tracks, while others travelled on the main line. At Corby, for example, BSC ran an extensive industrial system, with trainloads of two-axle tippler wagons hauled by ex-BR Class 14 diesel-hydraulics. On South Humberside, the North Lindsey Light Railway remained open for ironstone from Winterton until 1980. Among the main-line railheads for ironstone or haematite that survived in the 1970s were Banbury in Oxfordshire, Harlaxton near Grantham, Llanharry in South Wales and Beckermet in Cumbria.

However, imported ore was already well established at some BSC plants. In the Glasgow area, for example, block trains of two-axle hopper wagons operated from General Terminus Quay to Ravenscraig, hauled by pairs of Class 20s. In South Wales imported ore was railed from Newport Docks to Llanwern and Ebbw Vale. In North Wales and the Wirral, trains of bogie hopper wagons – similar in design to those that carried limestone for ICI – had been running since the early 1950s from Bidston ore terminal to Shotton. And in North East England, block trains of 56-ton bogie side-tipping wagons carried imported ore from Tyne Dock to Consett, latterly using double-headed Class 24 traction.

One of the first policy decisions by BSC after its formation in 1967 was to abandon the use of home-produced ironstone and haematite. BSC would save money by switching to foreign ores as they had a much higher iron content than the UK product and could be transported to UK ports economically in ships of more than 100,000 tons. The need to transport the ore within the UK would be limited because of BSC's decision to concentrate primary steel-making mainly at coastal locations. Nevertheless, the only BSC blast furnaces that were adjacent to a suitable deep-water port were those at Port Talbot and

Class 24 No D5104, later to become No 24104, passes Three Horse Shoes with Consett to Tyne Dock empties on 26 August 1966. *Ian Carr*

Some Clayton Class 17 locomotives worked freight duties in West Cumbria before ending their foreshortened careers in Scotland. No D8507 heads north from Whitehaven with haematite for Workington on 25 June 1968, while Nos D8520 and D8534 pass on the adjacent track. *Michael Mensing*

Nos 25275 and 25165 approach Bidston West Junction with imported ore from Bidston Dock to Shotton on 14 July 1976. At that time BR ran up to 15 ore trains a day between Bidston and Shotton. *Tom Heavyside*

Teesside – the other BSC plants would need some kind of overland transport link.

Road transport was not considered suitable because of the massive tonnages of ore involved. BSC considered pipelines but they would require a constant flow, which BSC could not guarantee. The railway, on the other hand, was well suited to this type of traffic. BR and BSC were impressed by the efficiency of the Quebec North Shore & Labrador Railway in Canada, which had been moving 12,000-ton iron ore trains since the 1950s. In the UK the tonnage per train would need to be more modest, but the same principle could apply

A pair of Class 20s, with No 8179 leading, heads north through Toton in July 1972 with 8E57, the 1135 Ashwell to Scunthorpe iron ore train. *Dr J. H. Cooper-Smith*

with fixed-formation trains of high-capacity wagons running between specialised terminals.

Unlike the 'merry-go-round' coal trains that BR had introduced in the 1960s, the iron ore would be carried in 100-ton bogie flat-bottomed tippler wagons with rotary couplings, avoiding the complication and expense of bottom door opening and closing mechanisms. The first wagon order was placed in 1970, and a fleet of several hundred vehicles was delivered between 1971 and 1977. Originally coded PTA for TOPS purposes (later changed to JTA/JUA), the tippler wagons were divided into four batches, each covering a specific route: Immingham to Scunthorpe; Teesside (Redcar) to South Bank and Consett; Port Talbot to Llanwern; and Hunterston to Ravenscraig. All were owned by BSC.

Nos 37301, 37302 and 37307 pass Gaer Junction with iron ore empties from Llanwern to Port Talbot on 12 July 1979. *Dr Michael Rhodes*

Infrastructure improvements for the new ore traffic included a new branch line into Scunthorpe steelworks, as well as conveyor systems and loading bunkers at the various ports. For the Consett flow, which started in March 1974, BR re-opened 3 miles of railway between Washington and South Pelaw in order to avoid using the busy East Coast Main Line or having to run via Gateshead. Even so, this flow was the least efficient of the new services, with trains limited to nine wagons because of the severe gradients and scheduled to take 2 hours for the 58-mile journey. Trains from Port Talbot to Llanwern, on the other hand, comprised 27 wagons and were the heaviest freight trains on BR at that time, hauled by triple-headed Class 37s with specially strengthened couplings.

The Redcar to South Bank ore traffic was short-lived, and the Consett flow ceased in 1980 following BSC's decision to concentrate its North East operations on the Teesside complex. The relatively young wagon fleet that had operated on those routes was sold to Procor and hired to Foster Yeoman and Amey Roadstone for aggregates traffic – echoing the transfer of the previous generation of iron ore tipplers and hoppers to sand and stone flows in the 1970s. Some of the ex-BSC wagons made redundant in 1980 are still used on aggregates flows at the time of writing, now carrying VTG number prefixes.

The Hunterston to Ravenscraig flow ran from 1980 – its start having been delayed by a protracted industrial dispute – until the closure of Ravenscraig in 1992. For most of its duration it used pairs of Class 37 locomotives, with a third locomotive added for the 1 in 77 climb between Mossend and Holytown on the outward journey. Only towards the end did single Class 60s appear. Although all the iron ore flows were designed to be self-contained, trains did occasionally operate off route if there were problems at a particular loading point. An example of this took place in 1990, when Ravenscraig received a number of trainloads of ore from Port Talbot – a distance of more than 400 miles. Another short-term off-route flow operated from Port Talbot to Scunthorpe in 2001.

The Port Talbot to Llanwern flow saw several changes of traction: the triple 37s gave way in 1979 to double-headed Class 56s, which in turn gave way to double-headed Class 37/7s and, finally, to single Class 60s. Further variety for a period in the late 1990s was provided by two Mendip Rail Class 59s, each of which was diagrammed to haul three out of the seven daily trains from Port Talbot to Llanwern. This gave EWS useful experience with General Motors traction ahead of the arrival of the Class 66s. The Port Talbot to Llanwern flow ended in 2001 with the closure of Llanwern's blast furnaces.

Nos 37137 and 37292 await departure from Hunterston High Level sidings with 6D14, the 1544 iron ore train to Ravenscraig, on 24 July 1985.

With Humber and Lindsey refineries visible in the background, No 60067 *James Clerk-Maxwell* approaches its destination with the 1442 Scunthorpe to Immingham iron ore empties on 29 October 1997.

The Immingham to Scunthorpe route was the first to use BSC's new rotary-coupled tippler wagons in the early 1970s and is the only such flow still operating at the time of writing. The double-headed Class 37s were replaced by single Class 60s in 1990, but in other respects the flow has changed little in three and a half decades. The ore originates in Australia and elsewhere and reaches Immingham in 75,000-tonne shiploads. Trains set out for Scunthorpe at approximately 90-minute intervals from Monday morning to Saturday evening, with up to eight additional trains on Sundays. The operation is an impressively slick one, with just 50 minutes allowed for the complete loading and reversing operation at Immingham.

5.

Metals

In the last 40 years the steel industry in the UK has changed dramatically, with production centred on a vastly reduced number of sites and with streamlined supply lines designed to increase efficiency. Throughout that time the railway has retained a large market share in the movement of raw materials and semi-finished products, together with a few specialised flows of finished products.

A new era for steel began in 1967 when the Iron & Steel Act brought the UK's 14 largest steel companies into public ownership as the British Steel Corporation (BSC). Those companies represented about 90 per cent of the nation's steel-making capacity, with major sites ranging from Ravenscraig in Scotland to Corby in the Midlands and Llanwern and Port Talbot in South Wales. In the early 1970s the Government approved a ten-year development strategy that would see major investment in new facilities, but also the closure of a number of loss-making plants and a 50% reduction in the total workforce.

The number of blast furnaces in the UK – representing the first stage in the steel-making process, producing molten iron from a mixture of iron ore, sinter, coke and limestone – shrank from 89 in 1967 to just 15 at the end of the 20th century, and those 15 were spread across just four sites at Teesside (Redcar), Scunthorpe, Llanwern and Port Talbot. Investment by the BSC included a new blast furnace at Redcar, which was first lit in 1979 and ranked as the largest in Europe with its capacity of 10,000 tonnes a day.

By that time all the country's surviving blast furnaces had completed the switch from using home-produced Jurassic iron ores to higher-grade, more economically produced ores from countries such as Australia, Brazil and Canada. The furnaces at Redcar and Port Talbot were located adjacent to deep-water ports, cutting out the need to transport the ore over land, while those at Scunthorpe and Llanwern received their ore by rail from Immingham and Port Talbot respectively. The high cost of transporting the ore was one factor that would lead to the closure of Llanwern's blast furnaces in 2001.

Back in the 1970s the BSC rationalisation programme included partial as well as total plant closures. In South Wales, Cardiff East Moors steelworks closed completely in 1978, while Ebbw Vale lost its iron-and-steel-making facilities in the 1970s but continued to manufacture tinplate until 2002. In North Wales the former John Summers works at Shotton lost its heavy-end iron-and-steel-making operations in March 1980, but retains secondary processing facilities to the present day, fed with semi-finished steel from the South Wales plants. Steel-making at Brymbo declined from the 1970s onwards and the plant closed completely in 1990.

In the Midlands, Round Oak steelworks closed in 1980 despite the large concentration of steel-based industries in and around the Black Country – evidently it was more cost-effective to transport the semi-finished or finished steel from larger plants in South Wales and Northern England than manufacture it locally. Corby works, where the Glasgow-based firm Stewarts & Lloyds had built England's most sophisticated integrated iron-, steel- and tube-making plant in the 1930s, stopped producing steel in 1980, but still manufactures tubes to the present day. In the Potteries, Shelton Bar works, which became the world's first steel

Above Two-tone green Class 47 No 1645 nears Magor with an up freight on 26 May 1970, comprising KYV coil carriers and assorted coal wagons. *Hugh Ballantyne*

Below Scunthorpe West Yard was the last automated hump yard to be built in the UK, opening in 1970. It was also the last to be closed, at the end of 1990. No 08401 shunts empty steel carriers towards the hump on 6 March 1990. *Dr Michael Rhodes*

plant using 100% continuously cast production in 1964, lost its primary steel-making capability in 1978 and closed completely in 2000.

In North East England the BSC cutbacks were largely concentrated on one location, Consett – the town that made the steel for the Blackpool Tower and Britain's most famous nuclear submarines. Consett works closed completely in 1980 with the loss of 3,700 jobs. On the other side of the country, iron-making at Workington ceased in 1981, but the works continued to roll rail from reheated steel blooms until production transferred to Scunthorpe in 2006.

The BSC rationalisation programme of the 1970s and early 1980s was followed by a period of relative stability. But in December 1987 the Government announced its intention to privatise BSC, and in September 1988 – after some 21 years in the public sector – the business was duly vested in British Steel plc.

Shortly after the sell-off the stability ended with a jolt as British Steel announced the closure of Ravenscraig, not only one of the biggest sources of

Towards the end of its life Ravenscraig steelworks dispatched slab instead of coil. No 90034 approaches Oxenholme on 21 July 1990 with 12 BAA wagons forming 6M24, the 0525 from Mossend to Dee Marsh Junction.

rail freight north of the border but also one of the biggest employers in the Central Belt of Scotland. The strip mill at nearby Gartcosh had already closed in 1986 and the decision to axe Ravenscraig was seen by some as a logical next step. Operations at Ravenscraig were wound down from 1990 onwards, with the last 1,200 workers leaving the plant on 27 June 1992 – just 35 years after the plant first opened. However, a small vestige of Scotland's steel industry survives at Dalzell plate mill, once closely associated with Ravenscraig but now supplied with slab from Teesside and Scunthorpe.

Since the privatisation of British Steel, two further changes in its ownership have taken place: in 1999 the company agreed a merger with the Dutch steel producer Koninklijke Hoogovens to form Corus, and in 2006 Corus itself was the object of a £4.3 billion takeover bid from the Indian company Tata Steel, the world's sixth largest steel producer. These changes highlight the inescapable globalisation of heavy industry.

Alongside British Steel/Corus, several independent producers have made their mark on the steel industry during the last 40 years. The biggest was Allied Steel & Wire (ASW), formed in 1981 through a partnership of British Steel and GKN. It used electric arc furnaces at its Cardiff

UK crude steel production, million tonnes/year		UK finished steel consumption, million tonnes/year	
1970	27	1970	17
1975	22	1975	15
1980	19	1980	13
1985	15	1985	12
1990	18	1990	13
1995	18	1995	13
2000	15	2000	14
2005	13	2005	14

UK crude steel plants, 2007

Location	Producer	Method
Port Talbot	Corus	basic oxygen converter (from iron ore)
Scunthorpe	Corus	basic oxygen converter (from iron ore)
Teesside (Redcar)	Corus	basic oxygen converter (from iron ore)
Aldwarke	Corus	electric arc furnace (from scrap steel)
Stocksbridge	Corus	electric arc furnace (from scrap steel)
Sheerness	Thamesteel	electric arc furnace (from scrap steel)
Cardiff	Celsa	electric arc furnace (from scrap steel)
Newport	Alphasteel	electric arc furnace (from scrap steel)

plants to produce sections, wire rod and reinforcing coil from scrap metal. ASW later acquired the Sheerness Steel plant on the Isle of Sheppey, which had opened in 1972 and used a similar process and manufactured similar products to those at Cardiff. Unfortunately ASW went into receivership in 2002, leaving more than 1,000 workers with no jobs and reduced pension rights. The Cardiff and Sheerness plants have since made a limited comeback, trading as Celsa Manufacturing (UK) and Thamesteel respectively.

The prospects for the UK steel industry will depend on the competitiveness of UK producers in the global market and on the level of demand for steel worldwide. There is little doubt that demand will increase, especially given the rapid economic growth of China. As for competitiveness, a strong pound made trading conditions difficult for UK producers in the late 1990s, and the UK became a net importer of finished steel products in 2001 for the first time in nearly 20 years. However, experts predict that the UK industry will make a gradual recovery, especially as Corus gears more of its production to the export market.

Scrap metal

Scrap metal is the principal raw material for those steelworks that use the electric arc furnace method to manufacture products such as reinforcing bar and wire rod in coil. Smaller quantities of scrap are used in plants using the basic oxygen converter method. Scrap comes from two types of source: 'old' scrap is derived from end-of-life products such as cars, and 'new' scrap comprises off-cuts and stampings from steelworks.

Until the 1970s scrap metal was moved throughout the BR network, with individual wagons being collected from dealers' yards or from public goods terminals and transported via the wagonload network to their destination. As a low-value traffic, scrap metal was a low priority when it came to investing in new rolling-stock. As recently as the early 1980s some scrap was still being carried in unfitted 16-ton MCO and 21-ton MDO mineral wagons, together with their vacuum-braked variants MCV and MDV respectively.

As BR wound down its traditional wagonload

Vic Berry's scrapyard on the former Great Central Railway in Leicester became renowned in the 1980s for its stacks of redundant BR locomotives and stock awaiting scrapping. No 08695 shunts 16-ton mineral wagons in the yard on 3 June 1981.

network, most of the smaller scrap flows transferred to road transport, especially in areas such as South Wales and the Central Belt of Scotland where the distance travelled was often short. However, scrap was one of two commodities – the other being coal – that BR continued to carry on its vacuum-braked wagonload network during the final year of that network between May 1983 and May 1984.

Sheerness Steel was the first company to invest in a fleet of air-braked PXA wagons for scrap metal. It introduced a fleet of 40 bogie wagons with a gross laden weight of 102 tonnes – quite a contrast to the traditional mineral wagons. The PXAs delivered scrap from various parts of the country using the burgeoning Speedlink network, as well as operating in trainloads from the nearby terminal at Ridham Dock.

A further lifeline for selected scrap metal flows came in 1984 when Standard Rail Freight Limited received a £2.52 million Section 8 Grant for the purchase of 160 new scrap-carrying wagons, fitted with air brakes and suitable for the Speedlink network. A single prototype wagon had entered service back in 1976, followed by an order for 20 further vehicles a few years later, but the 1984 order was a major step forward in ensuring that the railway would continue to carry scrap for the foreseeable future.

The Standard Rail Freight wagons were a two-axle open box design, with reinforced sides to limit the damage caused by swinging electromagnets. They were coded POA for TOPS purposes. All were deployed on traffic to the two United Engineering Steels (UES) works at Aldwarke and Stocksbridge (Deepcar), both located in the Sheffield district and served by trip workings from Tinsley Yard. Regular forwarding points were scattered across the BR network, from Workington in Cumbria and Stockton on Teesside to Snailwell in East Anglia and Silvertown in East London. In contrast to previous practice, each wagon was allowed no more than five days to complete its out-and-back journey, with a penalty imposed on any customer that caused that time span to be exceeded.

Scrap movements to Allied Steel & Wire

Left Embellished with Eastfield depot's 'Scottie dog' emblem, No 20127 is pictured at Ravenscraig No 1 yard on 24 April 1986 with the 6T12 scrap train to Shieldmuir. *Dr Michael Rhodes*

Below The United Engineering Steels exchange sidings at Aldwarke are pictured on 18 July 1991, with No 37509 coming off a short trainload of POA wagons.

(ASW) at Cardiff were the next to benefit from the introduction of air-braked stock. In 1987 ASW took delivery of 20 two-axle POA wagons, manufactured by Standard Wagon Ltd and nicknamed 'Black Adders' because of their all-over black livery. They were followed by a batch of 60 similar but slightly smaller wagons, also coded POA and manufactured by Powell Duffryn. The new wagons enabled ASW to increase its use of rail for long-haul scrap movements, including a

Right Scrap from Norton Metals temporarily brought life back to the Trafford Park Estates Railway. No 08423 negotiates the Trafford Park system with a trainload of POA wagons for Cardiff Allied Steel & Wire on 20 July 1989.

Below One of the last long-distance scrap flows to use vacuum-braked wagons was that from Halewood to Aldwarke. No 45126 passes Earles Sidings, Hope, with a mixture of MSV and MXV wagons on 28 August 1986 forming 8E41, the 1252 service from Halewood to Tinsley.

new flow from Norton Metals, which was made possible by the re-opening of the Trafford Park Estates railway in 1989.

Alongside the privately owned scrap wagons now in traffic, BR supplied a fleet of HSA vehicles, which were HEA (formerly HBA) hopper wagons with their bottom doors secured in the closed position as they would now be discharged by grab or electromagnet from above.

The HSAs appeared on various flows carrying shredded scrap steel to ASW Cardiff and from Corby to Clydesdale.

Despite the official end of wagonload traffic in vacuum-braked wagons in 1984, BR continued to use older stock such as MXV (formerly MCV) and MDV mineral wagons and HTV hopper wagons to convey scrap in full trainloads; routes where this happened included Snailwell to Cardiff and

Halewood to Aldwarke. Even more remarkable was the survival of vacuum-braked scrap wagons in mixed train formations from Skinningrove to Lackenby (Teesside) as late as 1989. Some MDV wagons allocated to Lackenby received air pipes – and were recoded MDW – so that they could travel with air-braked wagons without the need for a brake-van. But this mode of operation was unsustainable and, with no funding available for new stock, all scrap traffic to Lackenby had switched to road by the end of 1989.

The division of BR Railfreight into different business units led to the withdrawal of almost all steel-related traffic from Speedlink and the setting up of a metals network for selected less-than-trainload flows. This change took place in 1989, two years before Speedlink closed down completely. Some scrap flows could not be accommodated by the metals network, but others could be combined with flows of semi-finished and finished steel to form respectable trainloads on key

No 33053 awaits its booked departure time from Sheerness steelworks with empty scrap wagons for Willesden on 16 July 1987.

long-distance routes. However, the metals network turned out not to be cost-effective and was abandoned in May 1993. From that date, all rail-borne scrap traffic had to move in full trainloads.

The timetable for 1993/94 shows a rigid sequence of movements to each of three destinations, with optimum use of traction and rolling-stock resources. For ASW Cardiff, a single Class 60 locomotive collected trainloads of scrap from Leicester Braunstone Gate on Mondays, from Kingsbury and Saltley on Tuesdays, from Handsworth on Wednesdays, from Kingsbury and Saltley on Thursdays, and from Swindon and Exeter on Saturdays. Scrap for Sheerness Steel comprised a weekly train from Ridham Dock and up to three trains a week from Snailwell, all hauled by a Class 56 locomotive, which also covered movements of finished steel from Sheerness.

Scrap movements for United Engineering Steels had already been simplified in 1991 by running trunk services directly to Aldwarke instead of Tinsley Yard. From 1993 a single Class 56 locomotive diagram served Beeston and Tyseley on Mondays, Stockton on Tuesdays, Kingsbury and

Above A long-standing source of scrap metal was the Crossley Evans yard at Shipley. Hunslet 0-4-0 diesel-hydraulic No 42 *Prince of Wales* positions a single POA wagon for collection by BR No 37054 on 16 July 1990. This traffic was still operating in early 2008, with a weekly block train from Shipley to Cardiff.

Below A section of the former GWR Birmingham-Wolverhampton line remained in use to serve Bilston scrapyard. No 08616 shunts a single JXA wagon at Bilston on 21 February 1992.

Tyseley on Wednesdays, Shipley on Thursdays, and Kingsbury and Tyseley on Fridays. There was also a weekend trip from Aldwarke to Mossend and back for a temporary flow of scrap from Ravenscraig.

In the brief era when the bulk freight business was divided between Transrail, Loadhaul and Mainline Freight, the ASW traffic went to Transrail, the United Engineering Steels traffic to Loadhaul, and the Sheerness traffic to Mainline Freight. In 1995 Transrail won a new flow of scrap from Shotton to Port Talbot. This flow comprised off-cuts from the coil delivered to Shotton and was carried in a fleet of 15 102-tonne JXA wagons owned by CAIB, specially modified with hoods constructed from redundant tank barrels in order to prevent the lightweight load from escaping. The traffic was attached to one of the three daily trains that already ran between South Wales and Shotton.

In 1996 EWS took over all scrap flows previously handled by Transrail, Loadhaul and Mainline Freight. The company took ownership of the POA scrap wagons used for UES traffic; they were recoded SSA and subsequently rebodied. Meanwhile a new scrap metal customer, European Metals Recycling (EMR), appeared on the scene in 1997. EMR was the UK's largest scrap operator, processing more than 3 million tonnes a year for resale overseas. Following trial movements from Laisterdyke to Liverpool Docks, EMR invested £250,000 in a dedicated rail terminal for scrap metal at Alexandra Dock, Liverpool, which received three 1,000-tonne trainloads each week. The usual points of origin for this traffic in 1998/99 were Handsworth, Swindon and Attercliffe Road (Sheffield).

As EWS developed its Enterprise wagonload network, trainload deliveries of scrap metal were supplemented by wagonload traffic on various routes. Movements took place from St Erth to Liverpool, from Plymouth to Cardiff, from Kincardine to Cardiff, from Darlington to Liverpool, and from Pickering to Liverpool, the last-mentioned flow using the North Yorkshire Moors Railway. However, EWS scaled down its wagonload operations after the departure of its charismatic chairman Ed Burkhardt and opportunities to move smaller quantities of scrap by rail became more limited.

EMR continued to make extensive use of the railway, handling regular trainloads of scrap at Liverpool and receiving additional traffic at Tilbury Docks, where two weekly trains from Saltley were operating in early 2001, and at Tyne Dock. The wagon fleet for scrap traffic was boosted by the use of EWS-owned MBA 'monster box' wagons, which entered service in 1999. They appeared on various old and new flows, including trainloads of scrap from Beeston to Newport Docks for Simsmetal (UK) Ltd. That company received two Freight Facilities Grants to support its use of rail: £800,000 for track and handling equipment at Beeston in 2002, and £1.72 million for facilities at Newport Docks in 2003.

The long-established scrap traffic for ASW benefited in 2002 from the introduction of 26 new bogie JNA wagons; however, the flows to both Cardiff and Sheerness plants were interrupted soon afterwards by ASW's collapse. They resumed in 2003, but at a lower level than before the collapse. At Aldwarke, the traffic for British Steel Industrial Steels (formerly UES) continued to travel in trainloads from several locations including Stockton, Shipley, Beeston and Handsworth, and for a time it also received wagonload scrap deliveries from Corby.

The movement of scrap from Shotton to Port Talbot ceased following changes in the production process at Shotton, but in late 2005 EWS began supplying Port Talbot with scrap from other locations, including Laisterdyke, Handsworth and Swindon. New forwarding points for scrap were opened at Lincoln in 2004, Hitchin in 2006 and Brierley Hill in 2006. EWS's monopoly of rail-borne scrap traffic was broken for a time as Freightliner ran scrap trains from Hitchin and Beeston to Cardiff, the latter flow lasting until summer 2007.

At the time of writing EWS moves regular trainloads of scrap from more than a dozen locations to receiving points at Liverpool, Aldwarke, Cardiff, Port Talbot and Sheerness. The wagonload network conveys scrap from St Blazey to Cardiff and from Plymouth to Liverpool, while traffic from Mossend to Liverpool has been carried in a mixture of block trains and wagonload consignments. Most of the traffic now uses bogie JXA, JNA and MBA wagons, but many rebodied SSA wagons are still in traffic on services to Aldwarke and between St Blazey and Cardiff.

Semi-finished and finished steel

The railways have traditionally carried a vast array of semi-finished and finished steel products, ranging from pig iron, which is the solidified raw iron produced by a blast furnace, to steel plate for shipbuilding and steel pipes for the water, oil and gas industries. In general terms the need to transport semi-finished steel increased as the number of blast furnaces and continuous casting plants declined, requiring many steel mills to be fed with raw steel produced elsewhere. Conversely, rail-borne movements of finished steel have declined because of the disparate nature of the traffic, making it ill-suited to trainload operation.

Back in the 1950s the quantities of pig iron transported by rail were large enough for BR to build a specialised fleet of pig iron wagons, many of which were still in service in the 1970s. They were essentially low-sided open wagons of sufficiently heavy construction to withstand the force of lumps of iron being dropped into them by an overhead crane. A small amount of pig iron traffic survived into the Speedlink era, using a pool of SPA plate wagons that had been adapted by having the insides of their sides lined with angled wooden boards to protect the doors during loading. One of the last such flows was still operating to Pensnett, in the West Midlands, in the mid-1980s.

Where iron-making and steel-making take place in the same complex, the output from the blast furnace is transported to the steel-making plant as a liquid, at temperatures of up to 1,500°C. Rail movements of this molten metal require torpedo ladle wagons of massive proportions; those that operate over the Corus internal system from Redcar to Lackenby (Teesside) have a gross laden weight of 700 tonnes. For a short period from 1969 BR operated a main-line flow of molten metal, from Cargo Fleet (Teesside) to Consett, in order to boost the steel-making capability of the Consett works. For this traffic British Steel acquired six 246-tonne torpedo ladle wagons suitable for main-line running; the trains were subject to a 20mph restriction when loaded and were always double-headed to minimise the risk of a breakdown, leading to the metal solidifying.

Once molten iron has been converted into steel – a process in which the liquid is mixed with scrap metal, lime and oxygen – it passes through a continuous casting plant to produce one of three forms of semi-finished steel: a slab (a long, thick, flat piece of steel, with a rectangular cross-section), a bloom (a long piece of steel with a square cross-section) or a billet (like a bloom, but with a smaller cross-section). This range of products is well suited to rail freight because the quantities requiring movement tend to be large and regular.

Slabs, blooms and billets are the raw material for rolling mills, which make a range of semi-finished and finished products including plate, strip, wire rod, sections and rail. Steel strip is a thin version of plate, typically a few millimetres thick, which is coiled in order to make handling and storage easier; it is then known as strip coil or hot rolled coil. Hot rolled coil may then be transformed into cold reduced coil, a process in which the steel is pickled in hydrochloric acid to remove impurities, rolled to a smaller thickness, re-coiled, then either annealed to make it ductile again or galvanised to give it a protective layer of zinc. Both hot rolled and cold reduced coil are extensively transported by rail.

In the 1970s BR used a mixture of block trains and wagonload services to convey slabs, blooms, billets, hot rolled coil and various finished products. In most cases the steel was carried on specialised wagons. For long products such as billets, BR used mainly bogie bolster wagons of various types, such as the 30-ton-capacity Bogie Bolster C (TOPS code BCV/BCO) and the 42-ton-capacity Bogie Bolster D (BDV/BDO). These and other types of bolster wagon could also carry finished steel such as sections, reinforcing bars and tubes, as well as loads not related to the steel industry such as sawn timber.

Steel plate was carried where possible on two-axle SPV/SPO plate wagons, but BR also owned bogie plate wagons (BPV/BPO) for longer sheets of plate and trestle wagons for plate that was too wide to lie flat. The Trestrol type (BVV) was a low-floored well wagon with a trestle mounted on its floor; it could carry plate up to 13 feet wide compared with just 8 feet for a normal plate wagon. A few Trestrols remained in service at the

Left No 24063 passes Brymbo East box with empty plate and bolster wagons on 12 July 1976. Brymbo steelworks employed almost 2,500 people in the early 1970s, but rail traffic finished in October 1982 and the works ceased production in September 1990. *Tom Heavyside*

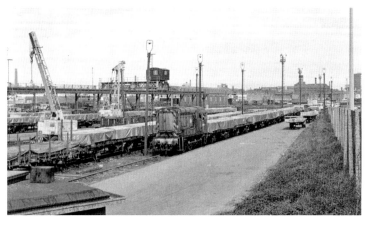

Above No 40193 passes Rotherham Road, on the former Great Central line between Rotherham and Swinton, with a mixed train carrying mainly wire rod in coil on 2 June 1977. The first vehicle is an STV tube wagon, followed by KRV and KSV coil wagons. *Gavin Morrison*

Left Walsall Tasker Street steel terminal is pictured on 8 April 1977, with No 08466 shunting a rake of sheeted pipe wagons. This terminal closed in the 1980s. *Michael Mensing*

end of the 1970s carrying plate for the shipbuilding industry. Another traffic type carried on SPV/SPO plate wagons was wire rod in coil; for this usage the wagons were modified with suitable cradles.

For strip coil BR used a wide variety of wagons, some purpose-built and others converted from different types such as bogie bolster, plate, pig iron and mineral wagons. All had some kind of cradle to carry the coil, which could be 'eye to end', 'eye to side' or 'eye to sky' depending on the wagon type, and some had nylon hoods to protect moisture-sensitive steel from rain damage. In the early 1980s more than 20 different types of vacuum-braked or unfitted coil wagons were in

use; many worked short-distance flows such as those from the South Wales steel plants to Cardiff Docks and from Scunthorpe to Flixborough, but examples could also turn up almost anywhere on the wagonload network. Some vintage BNX and BJV coil wagons remained in trainload use between Port Talbot and Swindon as late as 1987.

For movements of rail BR operated a fleet of 51-ton-capacity Borail wagons (BRV), which were 62 feet long – unusually long for a British wagon of that era – and could be used for other loads such as concrete beams and fabricated steelwork. Other specialised rolling-stock types for steel traffic were two-axle SOV pipe wagons, two-axle STV tube wagons and bogie BQV pipe wagons. The BQVs

Swindon Works sets the scene for No 37259 nearing the end of its journey with 6A44, the 0905 Margam to Swindon steel coil train, on 31 July 1987. The consist includes BNX and BJV wagons, all then approaching the end of their lives.

With hot rolled coil loaded 'eye to sky' on BAA and BBA wagons, No 37901 *Mirrlees Pioneer* approaches Wrexham with 6M44, the 0245 Severn Tunnel Junction to Dee Marsh Junction service, on 26 September 1987.

Locations on Teesside receiving and forwarding iron and steel traffic, 1978

Location	Customer	Traffic
Cargo Fleet	BSC	finished steel (out)
Cargo Fleet	Teesside Bridge & Engineering Co	finished steel (in)
Cliff House	Batchelor Robinson	scrap
		fabricated steelwork (out)
Cliff House	Shaw and Herring	scrap
Hartlepool South Works	BSC	various raw materials (in)
		pipes and plates (out)
Haverton Hill	Smiths Dock	plate for shipbuilding (in)
Lackenby	BSC	various raw materials (in)
		semi-finished and finished steel (out)
Middlesbrough	M. Baum & Co	steel for North Sea oil industry (in)
Middlesbrough	Cleveland Bridge & Engineering Co	steel for North Sea oil industry (in)
Middlesbrough	E. Pearson	scrap
Middlesbrough	Redpath Dorman Long	semi-finished steel (in)
		fabricated steelwork (out)
Redcar	J. Buckworth	steel stockholder
Redcar	BSC ore terminal	imported iron ore (out)
Seaton-on-Tees	Laing Pipelines	steel for North Sea oil industry (in)
Skinningrove	BSC	crude steel (in)
		finished sections and arches (out)
South Bank	BSC Cleveland Works	various raw materials (in)
		finished steel sections (out)
		ferro-manganese (out)
South Bank	Geo Cohen	scrap (in and out)
South Bank	C. L. Prosser	scrap
South Bank	W. G. Readman	finished steel (in)
South Bank	Redpath Dorman Long	semi-finished steel (in)
		fabricated steelwork (out)
South Bank	Smiths Dock	plate for shipbuilding (in)
South Bank	T. W. Ward	scrap
South Bank	Warner & Co	iron (in)
Stockton Millfield	T. J. Thompson	scrap
Stockton South	Coopers Metal	scrap
Stockton South	Head Wrightson Teesdale Works	iron (in)
Stockton South	Miles Turnbull	scrap
Tees Dock	Tees & Hartlepool Port Authority	finished iron and steel (out)

often ran in full trainloads, conveying pipes for the building of pipelines.

Three factors combined to transform the pattern of rail-borne steel movements in the late 1970s and early 1980s: BR withdrew or scaled down many of its wagonload services, forcing some customers either to sponsor trainloads or to transfer their business to road; vacuum-braked and unfitted wagons gave way to new air-braked types, usually allowing heavier loads; and British Steel restructured its manufacturing processes, leading to some traffic losses but also to some new high-volume flows of semi-finished steel between different plants.

BR's first production fleets of air-braked steel-carrying wagons appeared in the early 1970s. They included 300 two-axle flat wagons (SAA/SAB) and 305 bogie flat wagons (BAA/BAB), those with the B suffix having through vacuum pipes to allow them to travel in vacuum-braked trains. The two-axle variety did not last long in steel traffic; most were adapted either as container flats or as 'runners' to accommodate overhanging loads on a neighbouring wagon.

A second tranche of railway-owned air-braked steel wagons entered service from the mid-1970s onwards. It comprised nearly 600 BBA bogie flat wagons, similar to the BAAs but slightly longer, and more than 1,000 two-axle SPA plate wagons as replacements for the old SPVs. BR also fitted new bogies to the frames of old BDV wagons to produce a fleet of 1,250 air-braked BDA bogie bolster wagons, and carried out a similar conversion job on BPV wagons to create a small fleet of air-braked BPA bogie plate wagons.

The BAA/BAB and BBA flat wagons covered various trainload flows of semi-finished steel slab and strip coil that arose out of British Steel's 1970s rationalisation programme. The corrugated decking on the wagon floors aided the effective dissipation of heat from freshly cast steel blooms and coils; it also enabled the wagons to be loaded and unloaded by fork-lift truck.

Among the flows using the new wagons was the flagship 'Steelliner' service conveying hot rolled coil from Lackenby strip mill to Corby tube works, launched in 1981. This service was a model for the efficiency of modern rail freight, with each of two daily trains completing its out-and-back journey in less than 24 hours and conveying some 60 coils – increased to 80 coils from 1983. The gross load of 2,000 tonnes required double-headed Class 37 haulage.

Other major flows of semi-finished steel between British Steel plants in the early 1980s were: hot rolled coil from Ravenscraig, Llanwern and Port Talbot to Shotton; hot rolled coil from Llanwern and Port Talbot to the tinplate factories at Ebbw Vale, Velindre and Trostre; hot rolled coil from Lackenby to Hartlepool tube works; and blooms from Lackenby to Workington rail mill,

Shelton beam and section mills and Skinningrove special steels plant. The economies of trainload operation with these flows were doubtless a decisive factor for British Steel as it reorganised its production patterns.

Steel plants in the Sheffield and Rotherham areas, including the British Steel Stainless complexes at Tinsley and the United Engineering Steels mills at Aldwarke and Thrybergh, also generated a significant amount of semi-finished traffic, with some flows operating in trainloads and others using wagonload services via Tinsley Yard. Among the trainload flows were stainless steel slabs from Tinsley to Grimsby for export to Bremerhaven and rolling in mainland Europe; the same metal was later carried back in the form of stainless steel coil from Grimsby to Tinsley. The distribution railhead at Rotherham Masborough received trainloads of billet from Scunthorpe. In South Wales, BR won a high-volume flow of slab in 1984 from Port Talbot to the Alphasteel finishing works near Newport.

Alongside the inter-works flows, BR carried semi-finished steel to and from a number of ports and freight terminals. In the West Midlands, which was a major centre for steel-based industries but with no local steel-making capability since the closure of Round Oak works, BR operated six specialised steel terminals at Wolverhampton, Walsall Tasker Street, Wednesbury, Great Bridge, Brierley Hill and Kidderminster, each equipped with heavy-duty cranes and offering final delivery to customers by road. BR operated a similar facility at Sheffield Freight Terminal to serve the South Yorkshire market.

A challenge for BR in the 1980s was to increase its carryings of cold reduced coil, the moisture-sensitive steel that is sold to manufacturers of car bodies, domestic appliances such as washing machines, and many other industrial and domestic products. To make progress in this market, two potential barriers had to be overcome: a shortage of modern wagons providing suitable protection from moisture, and a shortage of suitable receiving terminals with covered handling facilities.

While most steel-carrying wagons were railway-owned, BR relied on leasing companies to provide new rolling-stock for cold reduced coil. The first type to enter service from 1979 onwards was a fleet

No 47332 passes through the disused station at Wednesbury Town with pig iron loaded on SPY plate wagons on 27 June 1977. This stretch of line between Bescot and Round Oak closed in 1993, while the line on the overbridge now forms part of the Midland Metro tramway. *Michael Mensing*

No 37293 approaches Over Junction, Gloucester, with 6V05, the 0915 Brierley Hill to Margam empties, on 15 February 1988. The load comprises seven Powell Duffryn PXA steel carriers from the then recently opened terminal at Round Oak.

of 105 wagons with telescopic sliding hoods, originally operated by VTG and coded PIB (later KIB/KIA) for TOPS purposes. The three-part sliding hoods provided excellent protection during transit and enabled up to two-thirds of the wagon length to be opened for loading or unloading at any one time. Further wagons of similar design were delivered in 1985, and they were joined in 1986-88 by 54 Powell Duffryn PXA (later JSA) wagons, which had non-rigid plastic sliding hoods instead of the metal type used on the VTG wagons.

A new terminal in the West Midlands with air-conditioned accommodation for cold reduced coil was provided in 1985 on the site of Round Oak steelworks. Privately operated by Round Oak Rail Ltd, the terminal dealt mainly with trainloads of coil from South Wales, supplemented by wagonload deliveries from other locations including mainland Europe.

Throughout the 1980s finished steel products such as sections, wire rod in coil, reinforcing bar, pipes and tubes were conveyed in a mixture of trainload and wagonload consignments. The West Midlands and Sheffield steel terminals dealt with finished as well as semi-finished products, as did privately owned distribution railheads such as Fogartys at Blackburn, D. & F. Steels at Leeds Stourton, A. V. Dawson at Middlesbrough, and Stockton Haulage at Stranraer. The last-mentioned terminal was developed specifically for exports of steel from Teesside to Ireland and received Scotland's first Section 8 Grant in 1979.

The division of BR into business sectors in the late 1980s brought various changes to steel traffic patterns, with Trainload Metals taking

responsibility for its own staff, infrastructure, locomotives and wagons. Many steel trains were now hauled by Trainload Metals Class 37 locomotives, including the experimental Class 37/9 variant, with smaller pools of Classes 20, 47 and 56 allocated to certain duties. The arrival of the first Class 60s in 1990 was eagerly awaited. A good example of operational efficiency was the use of the same locomotives and wagon sets on coil flows from Ravenscraig to South Wales and from South Wales to Shotton, with the wagons then returning empty from Shotton to Ravenscraig.

In South Wales, Trainload Metals was enjoying a period of investment and expansion. In late 1987 BR replaced the remnants of Margam hump yard by the new Margam Knuckle Yard at a cost of £1.3 million, its 18 through sidings providing a shared facility for British Steel and BR. In early 1989 new exchange sidings were provided at Ebbw Vale for inward coil and outward tinplate. New traffic in South Wales included hot rolled coil to British Steel's Orb works near Newport and reinforcing rod from ASW Cardiff for the building of the Channel Tunnel. On the debit side, Velindre tinplate works ceased production in 1989.

Trainload Metals transferred most of its wagonload steel traffic from Speedlink to its own discrete network in 1989 in an effort to contain costs and to increase accountability in the rail freight business. While this change resulted in some losses of marginal traffic, it also brought some improvements in transit times, such as through the introduction of direct steel trains from Lackenby to Blackburn and to the new Cobra railhead at Wakefield. However, it also resulted in some complex operations that can scarcely have been more cost-effective than Speedlink, such as a trunk service from Trostre to Whitemoor Yard that attached and/or detached wagons en route at East Usk Junction, Worcester, Washwood Heath and Whittlesea before continuing as a feeder service from Whitemoor to Snailwell and Ipswich.

One of the casualties of the withdrawal of steel traffic from Speedlink was imported coil from King's Lynn to the West Midlands, which could neither be conveyed in a viable trainload nor be combined with another less-than-trainload steel flow. The same fate nearly befell the port of Boston, but in the end Trainload Metals was able to reschedule the daily trickle of wagons into a weekly block train from Boston to Round Oak and Brierley Hill.

The year 1990 brought the news that Ravenscraig's hot strip mill was to close, presaging the total closure of the plant in 1992. The effect of the strip mill closure was to replace the existing flows of coil with a new flow of slab from Ravenscraig to South Wales, bringing to an end the triangular movements described above.

Marshalling yards were an obvious target for cutbacks as Trainload Metals tried to make its operations more cost-effective. Scunthorpe West Yard, BR's last operational hump yard, closed in 1990 after just under 20 years of service, while the

Above Tyne Yard remained in use as a staging point for block trains long after it lost its wagonload marshalling role. No 60031 *Ben Lui* leaves the yard with 6M71, the slab train from Lackenby to Workington, on 17 June 1991. Other trains visible are 6S46 from Doncaster to Gartcosh on the left and 6S66 from Tees to Falkland on the right.

Below Passing Rotherham Masborough steel terminal on 18 July 1991 is No 60005 *Skiddaw* with 6M47, the 1054 Lackenby to Corby coil train.

role of Tinsley Yard was reduced to that of a holding point for steel to and from the adjacent stainless steel plants.

The drive for cost-effectiveness did not stop with yard cutbacks. BR carried out a comprehensive review of its Trainload Freight business in 1992/93 as it sought to achieve an 8% return on its assets by 1994/95. The immediate outlook for steel traffic was not good: the economic recession had forced British Steel to reduce its output and the closure of Ravenscraig had resulted in the loss of 20% of all rail-borne steel traffic. That closure had brought just one new traffic flow, slab from Scunthorpe and Lackenby to Dalzell plate mill.

The Trainload Freight review concluded that most trainload flows of steel products and raw materials for steel-making were viable, but the less-than-trainload network established in 1989 was a heavy loss-maker. The decision was therefore taken to close down that network. Where possible, less-than-trainload flows were reorganised into block trains, but a few low-volume traffics were lost, such as tinplate from Ebbw Vale and Trostre to Wisbech and Westhoughton. Substantial savings were made by further yard cutbacks: Tees Yard closed as a marshalling location in early 1993, and operations at Cardiff Tidal Sidings were handed over from BR to Allied Steel & Wire.

Rationalisation in the West Midlands included the closure of three BR-operated steel terminals at

No 37197 approaches its destination at Wednesbury with 6M12, the 1230 Trainload Metals service from Cardiff Tidal, on 17 August 1989. The load comprises SPA and SEA wagons with reinforcing coils from Allied Steel & Wire.

No 08955 shunts steel traffic for Allied Steel & Wire at Cardiff Tidal Sidings on 16 July 1997.

Wolverhampton Wednesfield Road (an overflow for Wolverhampton Steel Terminal), Wednesbury and Great Bridge, with the sites being handed over to the Black Country Development Corporation. BR also closed the line between Round Oak and Bescot/Pleck Junction with effect from March 1993.

Meanwhile core trainload flows of steel benefited at last from the introduction of 16 Class 60 locomotives, complemented by 21 Class 56s and six Class 37/9s. The elimination of older, less powerful locomotives enabled an increase in tonnage per train without the need for double-heading. A typical payload per train was now 1,000 tonnes, compared with just 600 tonnes before the arrival of the Class 60s. Overall, Trainload Metals was now a leaner organisation, with resources well matched to traffic levels.

In 1994 steel traffic was divided on a geographical basis between Loadhaul, Transrail and Mainline Freight. The largest slice of business

went to Loadhaul, with an average of six daily trainloads of semi-finished steel from Lackenby and five daily trainloads of semi-finished or finished steel from Scunthorpe. Loadhaul also picked up the stainless steel to and from Tinsley, including a new flow of export traffic to Seaforth. Unfortunately the flow of export steel from Teesside to Stranraer ceased because it was not possible to sustain a viable trainload on that route.

Wolverhampton Steel Terminal lay in Transrail territory but became a Loadhaul facility because it received most of its steel from Lackenby and Scunthorpe. In 1995 Loadhaul invested £1.5 million in upgrading the terminal with an 80m by 30m warehouse, equipped with a 35-tonne gantry crane, enabling it to handle moisture-sensitive cold reduced steel coil.

Transrail handled inter-works traffic between British Steel plants at Port Talbot, Llanwern, Trostre, Ebbw Vale and Shotton, together with a single train from South Wales to the West Midlands, which carried tinplate from Ebbw Vale to Worcester and cold reduced coil from Llanwern to Round Oak. The terminal at Round Oak had been under threat of closure in 1994 but was now reprieved.

For Allied Steel & Wire, Transrail ran trainloads of imported steel from Hamworthy and finished products from Cardiff to Southampton, Brierley Hill and Wakefield, and the company used its Enterprise wagonload network to convey reinforcing bar and wire rod in coil from Cardiff and Sheerness. The Enterprise network also gave Transrail the flexibility to reintroduce tinplate traffic to Westhoughton and Wisbech, as well as a short-term contract to move rail from Workington to Tees Dock for export to India.

Mainline Freight had little involvement with steel traffic: it carried only occasional loads of finished product from Sheerness, alongside its inward flows of scrap metal.

The formation of EWS in 1996 brought all rail-borne steel traffic back under a single administration and it was not long before new

Wolverhampton was the most successful of the West Midlands steel terminals set up by BR, with both Loadhaul and EWS investing in improved facilities. Hot rolled coil is unloaded from a BZA wagon at Wolverhampton on 27 May 1998.

British Steel Lackenby sample programme, May 1995

Code	Dep	Days	From	To
6M78	0202	EWD	Lackenby	Etruria
6E34	0958	EWD	Etruria	Lackenby
6M13	0802	SX	Lackenby	Etruria
6E09	1544	SX	Etruria	Lackenby
6M87	1445	SO	Lackenby	Etruria
6E67	1240	SO	Etruria	Lackenby
6S58	0125	EWD	Lackenby	Dalzell
6E30	1515	MO	Dalzell	Lackenby
6E30	1332	MSX	Dalzell	Lackenby
6E30	1325	SO	Dalzell	Lackenby
6M58	0309	WFO	Lackenby	Blackburn
6E41	1253	WFO	Blackburn	Lackenby
6D19	0309	TThSO	Lackenby	Wakefield
6N67	0902	TThSO	Wakefield	Lackenby
6M01	2333	SuO	Lackenby	Wolverhampton
6M01	0001	MX	Lackenby	Wolverhampton
6E28	0710	EWD	Wolverhampton	Lackenby
6N30	1123	SX	Scunthorpe	Lackenby
6N30	1131	SO	Scunthorpe	Lackenby
6N06	1532	SX	Lackenby	Tees Yard
6N06	1525	SO	Lackenby	Tees Yard
6D11	1657	SuO+SX	Tees Yard	Scunthorpe
6N73	2100	SuO+SX	Scunthorpe	Lackenby
6D69	0222	EWD	Lackenby	Scunthorpe
6M28	0625	SX	Scunthorpe	Wolverhampton
6E31	1254	EWD	Wolverhampton	Lackenby
6M29	2241	SX	Lackenby	Corby
6E40	1030	MX	Corby	Lackenby
6M71	1525	SX	Lackenby	Workington
6E38	2148	SX	Workington	Lackenby

traffic flows began to appear, both for existing and new customers. EWS was particularly keen to regain a larger share of the finished steel distribution market. At Wolverhampton Steel Terminal, for example, it complemented the investment made by Loadhaul by doubling the size of the warehouse and providing a second 35-tonne gantry crane. By the summer of 1998 the terminal was receiving between seven and nine full trainloads a day, each with a payload of between 500 and 1,000 tonnes. The traffic included new flows of billet and bar from Roundwood, Thrybergh and Aldwarke, imported coil from Hoo

Junction and various East Coast ports, and aluminium billet from Lynemouth, which was delivered by road from Wolverhampton to Rogerstone in South Wales.

Maritime traffic offered EWS some good opportunities, with the tonnage of steel conveyed by rail from the East Coast ports rising from almost zero in 1994 to some 150,000 tonnes in 1998. At Hull, Associated British Ports (ABP) invested in Britain's first fully covered ship-to-rail transfer facility at King George Dock in 1997, built at a total cost of £3.4 million including a £2.5 million Freight Facilities Grant. In Kent imported steel

No 09025 shunts BDA wagons at Hamworthy Docks on 20 August 1987. The wagons would be loaded with steel from Ijmuiden for movement to Allied Steel & Wire, Cardiff.

Goole Docks saw a revival of rail freight in 1997/98 with flows of steel for import and export. No 56037 propels a mixed rake of BHA, BKA and IUB coil wagons towards the North Dock terminal on 7 August 1998 after working 6D50, the 0729 service from Rotherham.

from the non-rail-connected port of Northfleet was put on rail by Victa Railfreight at Hoo Junction for movement to Wolverhampton. On the other side of the country, ABP opened a covered steel terminal at Newport Docks in 1998, supported by a £2.5 million Freight Facilities Grant.

Smaller but nonetheless significant gains included the restoration of rail access to Goole Docks in 1996 after a three-year gap. A similar revival took place at Boston, where the first trainload of steel for more than four years left the port in October 1997. New accommodation was provided at Purfleet in 1997 for exports of billet

from ASW Cardiff. The rail link to Chatham Docks was restored in 1999 for flows of imported and home-produced steel.

At Immingham the opening of the Nordic rail terminal in February 1997 brought improvements to the two-way flow of stainless steel – slab out and coil back – between Tinsley and Sweden. The volume of traffic on this route increased from 180,000 tonnes in 1994 to more than 500,000 tonnes in 1997. The Nordic terminal handled a variety of other flows including exports of sections from Lackenby and Skinningrove, and imported coil to Wolverhampton, Round Oak and Llanwern.

Cold reduced coil is unloaded from BIA and BXA wagons at Immingham Nordic terminal on 7 August 2002.

EWS made renewed efforts to increase its carryings of cold reduced coil to the West Midlands and elsewhere. The key to progress here lay with the wagon supply, as it had done in the late 1970s. British Steel took delivery of 65 JSA telescopic-hood wagons in 1996, converted from redundant iron ore tipplers. A further 18 JSAs were converted from redundant aggregates wagons in 1998 for use by Round Oak Rail. EWS also invested in new rolling-stock by converting 42 BBA steel carriers into BIA/BWA/BXA telescopic-hood wagons in 1996, followed by the delivery of 260 new-build BYA telescopic-hood wagons from autumn 1998 onwards. The BYAs formed part of the huge EWS/Thrall Car wagon-building programme for which the former Adtranz rolling-stock factory in York was re-opened.

Armed with this enhanced wagon fleet, EWS increased its carryings of steel from South Wales to the West Midlands from 200,000 tonnes in 1996 to some 700,000 tonnes in 1998. It also began carrying cold reduced coil from South Wales to Carlisle and Wakefield, using scheduled Enterprise services. A new destination for finished steel within South Wales was the Impress Metal Packaging works at Rhymney, in the Cardiff valleys, which received three trains a week from October 1998.

In 2000 the Mersey Docks & Harbour Board opened a £3 million rail-linked steel terminal in Liverpool Docks. Its first traffic was coil from Lackenby, but in due course it handled steel plate and coil from South Wales and Shotton, using a combination of existing trunk metals trains and Enterprise workings. The Shotton to Liverpool traffic travelled via South Wales, which, despite the long detour – a journey of 400 miles in total – was a more cost-effective option than running a direct train from Shotton to either Warrington or Liverpool.

Pipe traffic was nothing new on Britain's railways, but EWS gave this part of its business a boost by creating a fleet of 30 BTA pipe carriers from BDA wagons in 1997. The BTAs had six sturdy stanchions on each side and could carry 15 pipes apiece, 50% more than a standard BDA wagon. These wagons were put to work on regular movements of pipes for the North Sea gas industry from Hartlepool to Laurencekirk, a flow that was still operating in January 2008.

EWS also carried pipes from Hartlepool to Leith for coating, and from Hartlepool and Leith to various destinations as required. A typical short-term contract in 1998 involved moving 40,000 tonnes of pipes for Transco from Leith to Bamber Bridge, Grantham and Yarwell, the latter on the Nene Valley Railway. The first of several campaigns of pipe trains to Georgemas Junction took place in 1996, while a much shorter-distance flow operated from Hartlepool to Tees Dock in 1998.

The pipe manufacturer Stanton, based near

Pipes were often moved under short-term contracts to temporary railheads. No 37682 passes Holme with 19 BTW pipe wagons on 10 October 1992 forming 7Z55, the 1000 from Leith to Carnforth. The pipes were for use with British Gas installations in Morecambe Bay; they had been coated with several inches of concrete to protect them and keep them weighed down on the sea bed.

The North Sea oil industry brought pipe trains to the Highland line on a number of occasions. Nos 37682 and 37517 approach Perth with 6X88, the 0635 from Hartlepool to Inverness pipe train, on 14 February 1997. The traffic would be worked forward the following day from Inverness to Georgemas Junction.

Toton Yard, returned to using rail in 1996 for fixed-term flows to various parts of the country. The first contract awarded to EWS saw pipes moved in block trains from Stanton to Plymouth for use by South West Water. Further contracts involved trains from Stanton to Immingham for export to Peru, to St Blazey for a drainage project on Bodmin Moor, to Redmire for Yorkshire Water, and to Hoo Junction for the Millennium Dome. Improved siding access at Stanton was provided in 1998, funded jointly by Stanton and EWS.

On the debit side, the closure of Shelton Bar works near Stoke-on-Trent in 2000 caused the loss of two trainload flows: slab from Teesside to Shelton, and finished sections from Shelton to Teesside. However, around the same time EWS

gained a new flow of sections from Teesside and Scunthorpe to Mostyn for export to Ireland.

Further cutbacks by Corus brought a number of significant traffic alterations in 2001/02. The closure of Ebbw Vale tinplate works spelled the end for inward coil and outward tinplate traffic. Lackenby stopped sending out coil, which meant that coil for Hartlepool now had to be sourced from South Wales – a much longer rail haul. Corby tube works also began receiving coil from South Wales instead of Lackenby, bringing to an end the long-standing 'Steelliner' flow launched in 1981. Lackenby meanwhile started supplying slab to South Wales, with up to three trains a day continuing until 2005.

The two-way traffic between Immingham and

The Avesta Polarit stainless steel plant maintained a rail freight presence at Tinsley Yard long after the end of hump shunting. The derelict tower and redundant lighting masts recall busier times as No 08528 trips a short rake of BVA and IGA wagons from the slab mill on 3 June 2004. This area of the yard has since been transformed into a warehousing and distribution complex.

Tinsley for Avesta Polarit (formerly British Steel Stainless) became more efficient in 2001 when EWS introduced a new fleet of BVA wagons that could carry both slab and coil, loaded on 'Lancashire flat' cassettes for ease of handling. However, the traffic became one-way only in 2006 when Avesta Polarit closed down its Tinsley rolling plant. The company had closed its rail-linked cold rolling mill at Panteg in 2004.

EWS boosted its share of export traffic from Scunthorpe in July 2002 by introducing intermodal trains to various ports including Felixstowe, Thamesport and Immingham, conveying wire rod in coil in ISO containers for export to South East Asia. The business grew rapidly and EWS celebrated its 100th train in December 2003.

Another EWS innovation was the introduction of 86 20-foot containers for domestic flows of small steel coils, enabling the company to break into a market sector previously dominated by road transport. The containers entered service in 2002; they were carried on FCA wagons and put to use on flows from South Wales to Round Oak and Middlesbrough.

The collapse of Allied Steel & Wire in 2002 brought an abrupt, albeit temporary, end to flows of wire rod in coil and reinforcing bar from Cardiff and Sheerness. This loss was doubtless a contributory factor in the closure of the Cobra distribution terminal at Wakefield in early 2003. Both Cardiff and Sheerness steel plants were

revived under new ownership, but outward traffic was slow to return. The Cardiff plant supplied materials for Heathrow Airport construction work in late 2003, with flows to Burton-on-Trent and Rotherham following in 2004. Sheerness produced very little outward traffic until block trains started operating to Rotherham in 2007.

Further rationalisation by Corus was announced in 2005, this time targeting its rail production operations at Workington and Castleton. Both sites would close completely, with Corus investing £130 million in a replacement casting mill and rail production facility at Scunthorpe. The new plant would be able to produce 120-metre lengths of rail, compared with a maximum of just 40 metres at Workington. The Workington plant therefore received its last trainload of slabs in August 2006, heralding the end of some 129 years of steel production at the Cumbrian site. However, that was not quite the end of the story: delays in the commissioning of the Scunthorpe plant meant that Workington continued to weld rail lengths imported from France until 2007.

A new flow of finished steel began in 2005 when EWS opened a distribution terminal at Bristol East, on the site of the long-abandoned Freightliner depot. The terminal handled sections from Lackenby and Scunthorpe, conveyed by trunk metals trains from the North East to Newport Alexandra Dock Junction (ADJ) Yard, then by a trip working from ADJ to Bristol. A second new metals service from ADJ began

No 66211 passes Middlesbrough with steel sections from Lackenby to Tees Yard on 1 June 2006. The train comprises BEA bogie bolsters and RRA spacer wagons.

Four different types of covered coil wagon – JSA, IHA, BYA and KIA – are included in this trip working from Llanwern to Newport Docks, pictured approaching East Usk Junction behind No 09105 on 6 June 2006. The Uskmouth branch curves round to the right.

operating in 2007, delivering imported cold reduced coil to Swindon for BMW Pressings.

Today the railway retains a virtual monopoly of semi-finished steel between Corus plants and a significant share of suitable finished product flows. At the time of writing 'the railway' in this context means EWS, as no other rail freight operator carries steel. The fact that most steel-carrying wagons are owned by EWS makes it harder for other operators to gain a foothold.

The key to successful operation in the future will be to increase efficiency by running longer, heavier trains and reducing further the need for shunting. EWS has already made progress in this area: in March 2007, for example, it increased the payload of slab trains between Port Talbot and Llanwern from 1,500 to 2,000 tonnes, which meant reducing the number of daily trains from five to four. Semi-finished steel traffic will always be vulnerable to changes in the industry itself: for example, much of Corus's output from Teesside is now destined for overseas markets, with little potential for long-haul rail movement in the UK. The best prospects for additional rail-borne flows are probably in the import sector, where the railway's share currently stands at less than 10%.

Non-ferrous metals

The most widely used non-ferrous metal is aluminium, its applications ranging from vehicle components and bicycle frames to cans, foil and other forms of packaging. Aluminium is produced from aluminium oxide, also known as alumina, which is the main component of naturally occurring bauxite ore. In the UK several aluminium plants have used the railway to carry raw materials and finished products in the last 40 years.

The Lochaber aluminium smelter at Fort William was opened in 1929 and became an important source of freight traffic for the West Highland line. After a modernisation scheme in the early 1980s Lochaber began to receive trainloads of imported alumina from North Blyth. The alumina was initially transported in former grain hopper wagons, but in 1987 a £1.1 million Section 8 Grant helped to provide new terminal facilities and 43 purpose-built PCA tank wagons.

One of the last freight workings to use unfitted stock was the alumina flow from North Blyth to Lynemouth. No 37048 shunts PAO hoppers at the Alcan import terminal at North Blyth on 17 July 1986.

The main outgoing traffic from Lochaber in the 1980s was aluminium ingots for further processing at Rogerstone works near Newport. This traffic was carried on Freightliner wagons and offloaded at Pengam Freightliner terminal for final delivery to Rogerstone by road. It remained with Freightliner after privatisation but the rail leg from Fort William to Coatbridge was not cost-effective given weight restrictions on the West Highland line and the need to hire Class 37 traction, and that section of the journey switched to road from June 2001. However, EWS won the Fort William to Rogerstone contract in 2005 and reverted to using rail from Fort William, with the ingots loaded on BDA/BEA wagons and sharing haulage with the alumina tanks between Fort William and Mossend.

The Lochaber plant was joined in 1971 by a new smelter at Invergordon, north of Inverness. For a time BR handled two traffic flows from Invergordon: aluminium blocks to the rolling mill at Falkirk, and imported alumina to Fort William. However, the Invergordon plant was costly to operate because it was remote from sources of power and it closed in 1981.

In North East England, Lynemouth aluminium smelter was opened in 1971. Its location took

Nos 37240 and 37403 *Ben Cruachan* **momentarily disturb the peace at Tulloch with the overnight alumina train from North Blyth to Fort William on 15 July 1992. The pair of locomotives would be split at Fort William, with No 37240 hauling the Corpach trip freight and No 37403 working a passenger service to Mallaig.**

advantage of local energy sources – collieries! It was also near the port of North Blyth, where alumina would arrive from Scandinavia and, later, Ireland. For the alumina traffic British Aluminium (now Alcan) acquired a fleet of 19 covered hopper wagons. Coded PAO, these wagons were the last batch of unfitted wagons built for use on the BR network; it was not considered necessary for them to have continuous brakes because their 8-mile journey was entirely on freight-only tracks. The PAOs remained in service until the early 1990s, when they were replaced by PCA tanks.

For many years Lynemouth dispatched aluminium ingots to Rogerstone on Freightliner wagons. A direct service from Lynemouth to Cardiff Pengam came into operation after the closure of Follingsby Freightliner terminal in 1987. The traffic then passed to EWS in 1997, which carried the ingots on BDA/BEA bogie bolster wagons. Initially EWS offloaded the traffic at Wolverhampton Steel Terminal, but in 2000 the rail leg was extended to Newport Docks, leaving just a 5-mile road connection to Rogerstone.

The Anglesey Aluminium plant near Holyhead was commissioned in 1971. Its huge demand for electricity – the plant has been estimated to use 12% of the electricity consumed in Wales – could be met from Wylfa nuclear power station. Anglesey Aluminium dispatched some of its finished product by rail until the demise of the Speedlink network, as well as receiving trainloads of petroleum coke until 2001. The rail connection was returned to use in 2005 for outward traffic in European-registered vans to Austria's biggest aluminium plant at Braunau am Inn; however, this traffic ceased in January 2008.

The Commonwealth Smelting (later Trident Alloys) works at Bloxwich in the West Midlands received zinc ingots by rail for many years. Until the mid-1990s the ingots were transported mainly from the Netherlands in European-registered vans. After 1997 EWS developed flows of Finnish and Norwegian ingots from Immingham and Grimsby respectively, using mainly railway-owned vans. The Finnish and Norwegian traffic reached Bloxwich via a combination of metals-sponsored and Enterprise wagonload trains.

6.

Petroleum

The consumption of petrol, diesel and other petroleum products in the UK soared after the Second World War as car ownership became widespread and as industry turned increasingly to oil as a fuel source. This growth provided BR with an ideal opportunity to develop the kind of siding-to-siding bulk freight that was promoted in the 1963 Beeching Report. The opportunity was successfully grasped: rail-borne petroleum traffic rose from 5.2 million tonnes in 1962 to 21.6 million tonnes in 1972. The oil companies and their customers established a network of regional railheads from which products were distributed by road. Some of the railheads were major installations, such as Leeds Oil Rail Terminal, which opened in 1967 with the capacity to handle 28 102-tonne wagons.

BR negotiated long-term contracts for petroleum traffic that required the customer to provide its own wagons, either by lease or by outright purchase. This policy ensured that the customer would be tied to rail and that wagon productivity would be high. From 1962 onwards the oil companies and wagon leasing companies acquired large numbers of 45-tonne two-axle tank wagons, taking advantage of the new 22½-tonne axle limit on BR. The early builds had vacuum brakes (later coded TTV/TTF), but from 1966 air brakes were adopted as standard (TTA/TTB). A further increase in axle loadings on many routes enabled the introduction of 51-tonne wagons (TUA/TUB) from 1972. The first production builds of 102-tonne bogie tank wagon (TEA/TEB) appeared in the late 1960s, gradually becoming the norm on many high-volume flows.

The earliest bulk petroleum trains were tame by today's standards, typically comprising just 15 two-axle tankers with a total trailing weight of around 500 tonnes. By the mid-1970s many trains were loading to 1,000 tonnes, with a few heavier workings on suitable routes. The next significant increase in train capacity did not come until the introduction of Class 60 haulage in 1990, when trainloads of 2,700 tonnes became possible subject to constraints such as the length of sidings and loops.

Having peaked at more than 20 million tonnes a year in the early 1970s, rail-borne petroleum traffic gradually declined to around 7 million tonnes in the 1990s. Several factors contributed to this decline. The two oil crises of 1973 and 1979-80 weakened the demand for some grades of petroleum, especially heavy fuel oil. Overcapacity in the UK led to several refinery closures in the 1980s, including Grain and Llandarcy. A growing national network of pipelines put paid to many long-distance rail flows: a pipeline is expensive to build but, once completed, its running costs are very low. The falling cost of road transport was another factor: many companies found it cheaper to run road tankers direct from refinery to end user and dispense with intermediate storage terminals. And finally there were exchange deals – agreements between two producers to swap a specified quantity of their product so that customers could receive their supplies from a refinery nearby even if that refinery was operated by a rival producer.

At the time of writing rail-borne petroleum traffic has stabilised at between 6 and 7 million tonnes a year. Most flows are now concentrated on a small number of routes and use specialised discharge terminals that have benefited from

The Langley oil trains regularly loaded to 16 bogie tanks in the early 1980s. No 47314 passes Ratcliffe with the 6E69 empties from Langley to Humber on 24 April 1984.

Twenty-seven TDA/TEA bogie tanks form 6E50, the 0940 Langley to Lindsey empties, on 18 February 1994. The traction is Class 60 No 60025 *Joseph Lister*, and the train is pictured pulling away from a crew change at Acton Main Line.

No 47222 *Appleby-Frodingham* passes LlanfairPG with 6E36, the 0740 petroleum coke empties from Holyhead to Humber, on 7 April 1988.

significant investment. The potential for additional exchange deals is limited and further refinery closures are unlikely. The greatest threat comes from pipelines and road transport, especially for flows over relatively short distances. However, the railway may yet be able to regain some business from other modes, depending on the extent to which it can reduce its costs without impairing service and reliability.

●

By far the biggest source of rail-borne petroleum at the time of writing is the Total/Fina Lindsey refinery at Immingham. Opened in 1968, Lindsey has a crude processing capacity of nearly 10 million tonnes per annum. In the early days Lindsey produced rail-borne flows to around 20 destinations, ranging from general distribution terminals such as Leeds, Kingsbury and Colwick to industrial sites such as power stations, chemical plants and steelworks. Even today it sends out around a third of its output by rail, with roughly 10 destinations served regularly.

Adjacent to Lindsey is the Conoco Humber refinery, commissioned in 1969. Humber has a slightly lower crude processing capacity than Lindsey and makes much less use of rail transport. Nevertheless, it is a significant rail freight location, with scheduled tank trains to several regional distribution terminals. Until 2001 Humber also dispatched trainloads of petroleum coke to Anglesey Aluminium at Holyhead, a flow that used a purpose-built fleet of PAB covered hopper wagons dating back to 1970.

During the 1980s a number of smaller flows from Lindsey and Humber switched from rail to pipeline, coastal shipping or road transport. The casualties included Torksey, Skellow, Liversedge, Ecclesfield, Darwen and Royston. However, the volumes on some of the remaining services increased as BR prepared for privatisation. A trial 2,000-tonne train ran to Colwick in 1988 with two Class 47s at the helm, paving the way for even heavier Class 60-hauled trains from 1990 onwards. Increasing the payload per train was essential if the railway was to retain a significant share of the petroleum market.

Despite the decline in overall petroleum tonnages, which made large numbers of wagons redundant, several new batches of bogie tank wagons entered service on Immingham traffic in the late 1980s and early 1990s. A notable design, because it broke away from the 102-tonne norm, was the fleet of Tiphook 90-tonne TDA tanks introduced in 1990. Another innovation was the use of a fleet of internationally registered TIA tanks from 1987, although their sphere of operation remained firmly in the UK.

After its formation in 1996 EWS continued to run trains from Lindsey and Humber to other general distribution terminals at Bedworth, Kingsbury, Colwick, Sunderland and Leeds, making full use of the haulage capability of a Class 60 wherever possible. The Immingham refineries gained a new high-volume flow to Jarrow in 1998, replacing the previous traffic from Stanlow. However, there were also some losses: Sunderland closed in 2001 and Leeds in 2002. In addition to the established flows, the terminals at Westerleigh and Theale received some deliveries from Lindsey in 2007.

EWS continued a long-standing service from the Immingham refineries to Langley carrying aviation fuel for Heathrow Airport and motor spirit for distribution in the London area. Having become more intense than ever in the mid-1990s, with 14 2,750-tonne trains each week, this traffic dwindled to nothing by 2003. However, aviation fuel for Heathrow continues to be railed from Lindsey to the terminal at Colnbrook, which was originally opened in 1990 for flows from Waterston and West Thurrock.

EWS operated single-product trains from Lindsey to a number of industrial sites, including the Rolls-Royce plant at Sinfin (Derby), Pilkington Glass at St Helens and Cleveland Potash at Boulby. It also supplied heavy fuel oil for starting the turbines at Drax, Eggborough, Ferrybridge, West Burton, Ironbridge and Aberthaw power stations. Sinfin changed its source of fuel in 2004 and Boulby no longer receives oil by rail, but Lindsey still supplies a number of power stations at the time of writing.

Bitumen traffic ran for many years from Lindsey to Preston Docks as part of a train that also carried other petroleum products. The other traffic ceased in 1992, while the bitumen to Preston Docks continued until 1995 as part of a train that also carried bitumen to Ashton-in-Makerfield. In 2001

Humberside petroleum train plan, October 1976

Code	Dep	Days	From	To
6M32	0018	SX	Lindsey	Preston Docks
6M43	0113	WO	Lindsey	Plumpton Junction
6L49	0137	MX	Lindsey	Liversedge
6M65	0205	MSX	Lindsey	Brownhills
6M65	0223	MO	Lindsey	Brownhills
6M35	0235	EWD	Lindsey	Kingsbury
6M30	0250	TFSO	Lindsey	Bedworth
6M30	0250	ThO	Lindsey	Bromford Bridge
6L42	0328	MSX	Lindsey	Leeds
6L42	0328	SO	Humber	Leeds
6L72	0328	MO	Lindsey	Leeds
6M42	0340	MWFO	Lindsey	Spondon
6L48	0407	WO	Lindsey	Elland
6L47	0407	WSX	Lindsey	Drax or Ferrybridge
6M58	0425	SX	Lindsey	Colwick
6M41	0500	MO	Lindsey	West Bromwich Albion
6L31	0518	EWD	Lindsey	Leeds
6M54	0530	SX	Lindsey	Colwick
6M49	0833	SX	Lindsey	Colwick
6M57	0908	SX	Humber	Kingsbury
6L32	0920	SX	Lindsey	Leeds
6J51	0935	SX	Lindsey	Ecclesfield
6D51	0955	SX	Lindsey	Thorpe Marsh
6L36	1123	SX	Humber	Leeds
6L33	1338	SX	Lindsey	Leeds
6L44	1450	TThFO	Lindsey	Skellow
6L45	1538	SX	Lindsey	Leeds
6L54	1811	SX	Lindsey	Leeds
6V68	2120	FSX	Lindsey	Langley
6D47	2224	SX	Lindsey	Cottam or West Burton

Left Several petroleum flows out of Immingham were operated by Freightliner Heavy Haul before EWS regained its monopoly of this traffic. No 66615 enters Elford loop with 6M00, the 1123 from Humber to Kingsbury, on 23 July 2004.

Right The long-awaited revival of the Preston Docks rail system finally took place at the end of 2004, with Sentinel shunters providing haulage between the exchange sidings and the Lanfina discharge terminal. *Progress* crosses the swing bridge with seven loaded TEA tanks on 20 July 2005.

a Freight Facilities Grant of nearly £2 million was awarded to re-open the Preston Docks branch; the re-opening was a long process, but in December 2004 EWS finally launched revenue-earning services. The Ashton-in-Makerfield terminal then closed.

EWS's monopoly of petroleum traffic was broken in September 2001 when Freightliner started hauling trains from Lindsey to Kingsbury, using two Class 66 locomotives from its recently formed Heavy Haul fleet. For a time Freightliner ran timetabled services from Lindsey to Colwick as well as Kingsbury, but the experiment came to an end in early 2005 when all petroleum traffic out of Immingham reverted to EWS. Total signed a five-

year contract with EWS to carry 11 million tonnes of refined products from Lindsey and a brand new a fleet of EWS-liveried TEA tank wagons entered service from 2006.

Alongside the outgoing traffic from Lindsey and Humber, BR hauled trainloads of crude oil from loading points at Tuxford and Gainsborough, initially destined for Llandarcy but later diverted to Immingham. The Tuxford and Gainsborough terminals closed in the 1980s, but a new crude oil loading point at Welton was connected to the network in 1985 and still produces EWS-hauled trains to Immingham at the time of writing.

●

Code	Dep	Days	From	To
		Humberside petroleum sample programme, July 1992		
6Zxx	0020	FO	Lindsey	Burn Naze
6M61	0130	SO	Humber	Bedworth
6V53	0220	SO	Lindsey	Langley
6M35	0230	MX	Lindsey	Kingsbury
6M31	0230	TO	Lindsey	Weaste
7M25	0240	MWFO	Lindsey	Ashton-in-Makerfield
6M11	0250	EWD	Lindsey	Colwick
6Z15	0305	MWO	Lindsey	Widnes
6M45	0320	MFO	Lindsey	Kingsbury
6V53	0420	MThFO	Lindsey	Langley
6M61	0519	TThO	Humber	Bedworth
6Z52	0745	TThO	Lindsey	Langley

The Shell refinery at Teesport produced rail-borne flows to various locations. The timetable for 1976 shows three daily departures from Teesport to Jarrow and less frequent services to Leeds, Eggborough, Ecclesfield, Deepcar and St Helens. The refinery closed in the 1980s.

Two further railheads on Teesside forwarded petroleum traffic in BR days: Haverton Hill (ICI) and Port Clarence (Phillips). For many years Haverton Hill produced a flow to the British Tar Products terminal at Glazebrook, while Port Clarence supplied railheads at Long Eaton, Bromsgrove, Weaste and Leeds. The Phillips traffic used an unusual fleet of TEA bogie wagons with barrels incorporating a sunken central section between the bogies in order to increase capacity.

By the mid-1990s the traffic from Haverton Hill had ceased and the receiving terminals at Long Eaton and Bromsgrove had closed. The last tank train to Weaste ran in June 1998 and the nearby terminal at Glazebrook, latterly served from Port Clarence, received its last delivery in late 1999. The Port Clarence operation was later taken over by Petroplus, which developed flows to Westerleigh and Bedworth and introduced new red-liveried TEA wagons in 2002/03.

EWS ran a small number of fuel oil trains from Seal Sands in the early 2000s, serving power stations at West Burton, Ferrybridge and Eggborough.

●

The Carless refinery in Harwich processes condensate from the North Sea gas fields on behalf of major gas producers. A loading terminal for the condensate was provided at North Walsham, with block tank trains operating from North Walsham to Harwich. This traffic continued in the 1990s under Mainline Freight then EWS management, but switched to GB Railfreight in 2005. The two-axle tank wagons used on this train were replaced in 2001 by 20 new TEA bogie tanks with Petrochem Carless branding.

Outgoing traffic from Harwich refinery in the 1980s included tankloads of refined solvent to Bow and Longport. The Longport traffic survived as a block train after the end of Speedlink in 1991 and reverted to wagonload (Enterprise) operation in 1998; it ceased in 2001. BR also carried tankloads of mud oil for the North Sea oil industry

from Harwich to Aberdeen Guild Street, using Speedlink until 1991, followed by a period of block trains, then back to wagonload (Enterprise) operation in 1997. GB Railfreight took over the mud oil traffic in 2005; it was diverted to terminate at Aberdeen Waterloo in early 2008.

●

Oil storage and refining at Thames Haven on the north bank of the Thames estuary has a history going back to the early 20th century. Two adjacent refineries were in operation in the 1960s: Mobil at Coryton and Shell at Shell Haven. Both provided significant volumes of rail freight on the Thames Haven branch, which had closed to regular passenger traffic in 1958. Operations were focused on Ripple Lane yard, with trip workings running between Ripple Lane and the two refineries and a network of longer-distance trains serving individual discharge terminals. BR carried a range of refined products from both refineries, including petrol, diesel, heating oil, aviation fuel and bitumen.

BR also ran loaded trains from a number of oil storage depots between Barking and Tilbury, which received their supplies either by ship or by pipeline. Those depots producing traffic in the 1980s included Thames Matex at Purfleet, Powell Duffryn at Purfleet and Unitank at Grays.

Most of the discharge terminals served from North Thamesside were located in East Anglia and South East England, although in the 1980s BR also ran block bitumen trains further afield to Kilnhurst in South Yorkshire and Four Ashes in Staffordshire. A particularly complex operation was the delivery of heating oil to nine distribution terminals on the Southern Region: Canterbury West, High Brooms, Galley Hill, Selsdon, Earlswood, Horsham, Chichester, North Camp and Staines. Each of these terminals received infrequent deliveries, typically ranging from once weekly in winter to once monthly in summer. The Canterbury terminal was served by Speedlink, while the other eight terminals were all served by dedicated trains. For reasons of railway geography Selsdon and Staines were served directly from Ripple Lane, but traffic for the remaining six terminals was staged at Redhill, with an overnight train running between Ripple Lane and Redhill three or four times a week.

PETROLEUM

The Thames Haven branch was once busy with tank trains to and from Shell Haven and Coryton refineries. No 47124 heads west along the branch with 7R71, the 1350 Thames Haven to Ripple Lane service, on 20 February 1987.

The staging sidings at Ripple Lane East are pictured on 22 December 1987, with No 37889 in charge of 6V52, the 1445 departure to Langley, and sister loco No 37893 waiting with 6M32, the 1501 departure to Thame. The Trainload Petroleum servicing depot is visible in the background.

Taylors Lane power station received fuel oil by rail for a brief spell in 1990. No 37706 sets back past Neasden Junction box with 6Z83, the 0915 from Ripple Lane to Taylors Lane, on 30 October 1990.

The Southern Region heating oil trains produced some unusual combinations of traction and rolling-stock. Electro-diesels Nos 73105 and 73118 enter Tonbridge yard with 6Y55, the 0556 from Redhill to Canterbury West, on 20 April 1990. The train will be split here, with portions going forward to Canterbury and High Brooms.

In the late 1980s BR identified North Thamesside petroleum as an ideal target for trying out the sub-sector dedication of resources, which would soon become the norm on the whole network. Accordingly most trains were hauled by a dedicated pool of Trainload Petroleum-liveried Class 37/7 locomotives from late 1987, with day-to-day maintenance carried out at Ripple Lane depot and a specific link of drivers allocated to the traffic. For a time traffic volumes held up well; new services operated to Glazebrook and Theale together with additional trains to Micheldever and Thame. However, the optimism turned out to be short-lived as competition from pipelines and direct road deliveries began to bite.

The combination of infrequent deliveries, limited terminal capacities and complex operating arrangements made the Southern Region heating oil trains particularly vulnerable. Already a small terminal at Ore, with the capacity for only 11 two-axle wagons, had closed in the 1980s. BR attempted to reduce costs in 1990 by cutting out the Redhill staging post, but to no avail: Staines and Galley Hill lost their service in 1991 and 1992 respectively and the other heating oil terminals – Canterbury West, High Brooms, Galley Hill, Earlswood, Horsham, Chichester and North Camp – closed in 1993. That year also brought the end of rail loading at Shell Haven refinery, foreshadowing the refinery's complete closure in 1999.

By the time Mainline Freight was formed in 1994 the only regular petroleum flows from North Thamesside were three trains a week from Coryton to Kilnhurst and occasional trains of fuel oil from Coryton to distribution terminals at Cambridge (Brooklands Avenue) and Norwich.

Thomas Hill 0-4-0 diesel-hydraulic No 26 stands in the loading sidings at Shell Haven refinery on 31 October 1990. By this time rail traffic from Shell Haven was in sharp decline.

PETROLEUM

Infrequent deliveries of heating oil kept a token freight presence on several Southern Region lines that otherwise saw nothing but multiple-units. One of the last workings of 6L44 from Portfield siding, near Chichester, begins its journey to Thames Haven behind No 47379 on 17 February 1993.

The oil depot at Micheldever handled a long-standing flow from Thames Haven, with additional deliveries coming on stream from Waterston in 1989. Nos 37220 and 37294 shunt TEA tanks at Micheldever on 13 August 1990 after bringing in 6Z38, the 2135 departure from Waterston.

North Thamesside petroleum train plan, May 1978

Code	Dep	Days	From	To
6M28	0109	TSO	Ripple Lane	Willesden
6V32	0235	TThO	Ripple Lane	Exeter
6V32	0235	WFO	Ripple Lane	Westbury
6O45	0250	MSX	Ripple Lane	Norwood
6O45	0250	SO	Ripple Lane	Salfords
6M31	0300	MSX	Ripple Lane	Rowley Regis
6M72	0345	SX	Ripple Lane	Rugeley
6M43	0358	MSX	Ripple Lane	Hawkesbury Lane
6O46	0400	SX	Grays	Micheldever
6B47	1430	WSX	Ripple Lane	Royston
6V21	1435	FO	Ripple Lane	Bristol
6M51	1910	MWFO	Ripple Lane	Kingsbury
6M39	1910	TThO	Ripple Lane	Corby
6L34	1955	MWThO	Ripple Lane	Cambridge
6V43	1955	TO	Purfleet	Southall
6V86	2055	MO	Ripple Lane	Southall
6V58	2055	WFO	Ripple Lane	Didcot
6V44	2055	FSX	Purfleet	Colnbrook
6O42	2133	TFO	Purfleet	Fawley
6M70	2250	MFO	Ripple Lane	Ince & Elton
6N46	2325	MTWO	Ripple Lane	Norwich

Ripple Lane yard had ceased to act as a staging point in 1992, so all trains now ran directly between Coryton and their final destination.

Under EWS management, a revival of traffic from Coryton took place, with trains operating in 1997/98 to Langley, Ipswich, Barnwell Junction (instead of Brooklands Avenue), Littlemore, Rugeley, Brownhills, Whittington, Lostock and Ferrybridge. However, the long-standing bitumen flow to Kilnhurst ceased in 1998 and all the flows won in 1997/98 had gone by early 2003. All that remained after that was bitumen from Coryton to Llandarcy, a flow that started in 1999 following the closure of Llandarcy refinery. At the time of writing the Coryton to Llandarcy traffic is the sole user of the Thames Haven branch; it shares haulage between Ripple Lane and Newport with Ford automotive traffic in order to maximise the use of resources.

●

The BP refinery at Grain was a major source of rail freight in the 1970s. Frequent trip workings operated between Grain and Hoo Junction yard and trunk trains ran from Hoo Junction to a range of destinations including Brookgate, Dover, Richborough, Ore, Galley Hill, Horsham, Earlswood, Selsdon, Staines, Southall, Slough, Earley, Thatcham, Thame and Oxford. After the refinery closed, Grain became an oil storage depot and dispatched trains of aviation fuel to Stansted and gas oil to BR fuelling points in the 1980s. Grain also received bitumen from Llandarcy, a flow that continued until 1999.

●

The Esso refinery at Fawley was opened in 1949. It expanded rapidly in the 1950s and operates today with a capacity of 15.6 million tonnes of crude oil per year. Fawley relied heavily on rail freight in the 1960s and generated BR's heaviest train of the period: a 54-wagon working to Bromford Bridge. However, much of the core business went over to pipelines in the 1970s, with direct pipeline links to distribution terminals at West London, Purfleet,

North Thamesside petroleum train plan, October 1990

Code	Dep	Days	From	To
6O45	0111	MX	Ripple Lane	Redhill
6P46	0205	FO	Ripple Lane	Norwich
6V06	0308	SX	Ripple Lane	Frome
6M22	0314	TO	Ripple Lane	Weaste
6V09	0340	WO	Ripple Lane	Theale
6H34	0410	MFSX	Ripple Lane	Cambridge
6Oxx	0420	FO	Ripple Lane	Canterbury
6Oxx	0420	WO	Ripple Lane	Chichester
6Oxx	0420	TO	Ripple Lane	Galley Hill
6O51	0523	MX	Ripple Lane	Micheldever
6E32	0558	FO	Ripple Lane	Watton-at-Stone
6V54	0732	ThO	Ripple Lane	Didcot
6V54	0732	WFO	Ripple Lane	Banbury/Oxford
6Oxx	0732	TO	Ripple Lane	North Camp
6Oxx	0807	Q	Ripple Lane	Earlswood
6Oxx	0807	Q	Ripple Lane	Horsham
6O53	0910	MO	Ripple Lane	Selsdon
6Oxx	0930	Q	Ripple Lane	Eastleigh
6O36	1010	MO	Ripple Lane	Staines
6E31	1041	Q	Ripple Lane	Barnwell Jn/Peterborough
6O64	1110	MO	Ripple Lane	Micheldever
6V22	1130	MO	Ripple Lane	Slough/Southall
6V33	1338	SX	Ripple Lane	Thame
6V18	1901	SX	Ripple Lane	Old Oak Common
6M81	2025	ThO	Ripple Lane	Four Ashes
6E62	2259	MWFO	Ripple Lane	Kilnhurst
6Zxx	2315	Q	Ripple Lane	Bridgwater/Llanwern/Hereford

Q = as required

Avonmouth, Birmingham, Nottingham and Manchester.

By the mid-1980s the BR timetable included just five loaded block trains a week out of Fawley: a twice-weekly trainload of liquefied petroleum gas (LPG) to Longport, a weekly LPG train to Clydach, a weekly bitumen train to Kilnhurst, and a weekly bitumen train to Cardiff. Less-than-trainload traffic to other destinations used the Speedlink network. In the inward direction, crude oil from the Wytch Farm oilfield at Furzebrook justified two trainloads a day, with additional deliveries from Micheldever as required. These flows were joined by crude oil from a new loading point at Holybourne in 1986, amounting to three trains a week.

In 1990 expansion of the Wytch Farm oilfield led to the loss of the crude oil traffic from Furzebrook to Fawley in favour of a pipeline, but in its place BR gained two trains a day of naturally occurring LPG from Furzebrook to Avonmouth for onward distribution by road. The frequency of the LPG trains was halved in 1999 when BP started re-injecting more of the gas into the ground in order to keep the remaining oil reserves under pressure, and the traffic ceased altogether in 2005.

In the 1994 carve-up of BR Trainload Freight, all Fawley traffic was allocated to Mainline

A quaint survival was the small Esso oil terminal at Shrewsbury Abbey. Its supplies were loaded on rail at Bromford Bridge and conveyed to Shrewsbury by Speedlink services. No 08390 shunts the Abbey terminal on 22 August 1985.

The BP terminal at Furzebrook was a loading point for crude oil until its conversion to an LPG terminal. No 47156 shunts TEA tanks at Furzebrook on 20 August 1987 before working the morning train to Fawley.

Freight, which operated seven loaded trains a week out of the refinery – three trains with bitumen for Plymouth Cattewater and gas oil for fuelling points in South West England, and four trains destined for the West Midlands with gas oil for railway fuelling points, LPG for Longport and bitumen for Bromford Bridge. EWS continued to operate both trunk trains but lost the Longport LPG traffic in favour of road haulage from Stanlow in 1997.

Today, less than 5% of Fawley's production is distributed by rail, comprising bitumen to Bromford Bridge and gas oil to railway fuelling points. Crude oil continues to be delivered from Holybourne.

BR carried petroleum from a cluster of oil refineries in the Milford Haven district: Herbrandston (Esso) opened in 1960, Waterston (Gulf, later Petroplus) in 1968, and Robeston (Amoco, later Murco/Elf) in 1973. Early traffic from Herbrandston included block trains to Sighthill and Coleshill as well as wagonload movements via Margam Yard. However, Herbrandston had a relatively short life and closed in 1983.

Waterston and Robeston refineries remained busy in the 1980s with rail traffic to major inland distribution terminals such as Kingsbury and West Bromwich and to industrial destinations such as Llanwern steelworks and Didcot and Aberthaw power stations. In 1990 BR introduced Class 60 haulage on key services from Waterston and

Fawley train plan, January 1976

Code	Dep	Days	From	To
6T31	0130	WSO	Fawley	Hilsea
6V74	0308	MX	Fawley	Langley
6M52	0350	MX	Fawley	Longport
6M43	0655	FO	Fawley	Bromford Bridge
6Y63	0740	SX - Q	Fawley	Waddon Marsh
6V04	0740	SX - Q	Fawley	Oxford
6V71	0948	SX	Fawley	Tiverton Junction
6M39	1100	SX	Fawley	Longport
6V54	1120	SO	Fawley	Bristol
7B12	1320	SX	Fawley	Eastleigh
6V49	1444	MThO	Fawley	Oxford
6V95	1444	TFO	Fawley	Old Oak Common
6M29	1444	WO	Fawley	Willesden
6Y55	1612	SX	Fawley	Salfords
7B06	2045	SX - Q	Fawley	Eastleigh
6V77	2258	MWFO	Fawley	Cardiff
6V77	2258	TThO	Fawley	Plymouth
6E42	2325	MWO	Fawley	Ripple Lane
6E50	2325	TThFO - Q	Fawley	Hertford East

Q = as required

Robeston, including a new flow to Colnbrook for Heathrow Airport, making 2,000-tonne-plus trainloads the norm. Bucking the trend of terminal closures, Murco opened a new regional distribution railhead at Westerleigh in 1991, capable of handling 34 102-tonne tank wagons at a time.

Transrail took over the flows from Waterston and Robeston in 1994. It won a five-year contract with Murco for 11 trains a week to Westerleigh and Theale, but on the debit side aviation traffic to Colnbrook ceased temporarily in 1994 and the small distribution terminal at Heathfield closed in 1995 in favour of coastal shipping from Milford Haven to Plymouth.

Deliveries from Robeston to Colnbrook resumed under EWS management in 1997

Many trains to and from Waterston ran at night, but a regular daytime working was 6M50, the 1530 departure to West Bromwich Albion. This service is pictured leaving the refinery on 10 July 1985 behind No 47032.

No 33043 passes Hawkeridge Junction with empty petroleum tanks from Melksham to Westbury on 29 July 1982.

alongside the existing traffic to Westerleigh and Theale. Waterston was less fortunate: refining ceased in 1997 and residual rail traffic from the refinery site ended in 1999. At the time of writing Robeston has a schedule of five trains a week to Westerleigh and three to Theale, together with an 'as required' path to Bedworth. The traffic uses several designs of bogie tank wagon, including a pool of VTG-owned TEAs built as recently as 2006.

Llandarcy refinery opened in 1921 and was therefore already a well-established source of oil traffic in the 1960s. The timetable for 1968 shows scheduled departures from Llandarcy to Llanwern, Melksham, Swindon, Rowley Regis and Angerstein Wharf. However, traffic later declined and the only flows remaining by the early 1990s were two trains a week of bitumen to Grain and occasional trainloads of heated fuel oil to Llanwern. Refining at Llandarcy ceased in 1999, although the site continued to see tank trains with deliveries of bitumen from Coryton.

The Minimet (later Fuel & Marine Marketing)

oil storage depot at Cardiff Docks provided BR with regular flows to various industrial locations. In 1994 Minimet was sending trains to Didcot and Aberthaw power stations, Cowley Hill and Ravenhead (St Helens) glassworks, and Llanwern steelworks. EWS continued to convey oil from Cardiff Docks, with occasional trains running to Rugeley power station until 2006.

●

Stanlow refinery in the 1960s was one of the biggest sources of rail freight in North West England. The refinery had been developed by Shell after the Second World War on a site previously used for oil storage; BR secured contracts for numerous trainload flows, including long-distance workings to terminals such as Salfords for Gatwick Airport and Bishopbriggs in the Central Belt of Scotland. The Salfords traffic was conveyed in 1,600-tonne trainloads at a time when the norm was around 1,000 tonnes. Unfortunately this flow fell victim to the opening of a new pipeline in 1984.

In July 1987 Stanlow became one of the first examples of sub-sector resource dedication on BR. A pool of 13 Class 47 locomotives was allocated to Crewe for Stanlow and Ellesmere Port traffic. The

West Wales petroleum train plan, May 1983

Code	Dep	Days	From	To
6B05	0025	TO	Waterston	Newton Abbot
6A37	0045	TO	Herbrandston	Thatcham
6M27	0200	WO	Herbrandston	West Bromwich Albion
6A08	0300	MWFO	Robeston	Langley
6C15	0355	WO	Herbrandston	Uskmouth
6C19	0355	TO	Herbrandston	Hereford
6A18	0520	SX	Robeston	Theale
6A55	0655	MWFO	Robeston	Kingsbury
6B13	0700	MWO	Llandarcy	Bristol Bath Road
6C23	0700	FO	Llandarcy	Severn Tunnel Junction
6M34	0800	WSX - Q	Llandarcy	Thame
6A21	0800	WSX - Q	Llandarcy	Southall
6C62	0915	MSX	Llandarcy	Aberthaw
7C04	1340	SX - Q	Waterston	Haverfordwest (wagonload)
7C14	1335	SX - Q	Herbrandston	Haverfordwest (wagonload)
6C03	1435	MTThO	Llandarcy	Llanwern
6M50	1545	SX	Waterston	West Bromwich Albion
6A40	1545	MO	Llandarcy	Didcot
6O86	1645	TFO	Llandarcy	Dover Town
7E47	1800	MTThO	Llandarcy	Gainsborough (crude oil empties)
7E47	1800	WO	Llandarcy	Tuxford (crude oil empties)
6M47	2045	MO	Robeston	Holywell Junction
6M56	2125	TWThO	Robeston	Oakleigh
6O51	2300	TO	Robeston	Micheldever

Q = as required

West Wales petroleum sample programme, September 1992

Code	Dep	Days	From	To
6B13	0540	SX	Robeston	Westerleigh
6O39	0700	TThFO	Llandarcy	Grain
6Z62	0815	TThO	Llandarcy	Aberthaw
6Z62	1325	MWFO	Llandarcy	Llanwern
6Z18	2000	SuO	Robeston	Bedworth
6C30	2230	MO	Waterston	Heathfield
6M51	2245	Su+MSX	Waterston	Glazebrook
6O50	2320	SuWO	Waterston	Micheldever
6A14	2335	Su+SX	Robeston	Theale
6A15	2355	Su+FSX	Waterston	Colnbrook
6A15	2355	FO	Waterston	Langley

fleet was gradually repainted into the new Trainload Petroleum livery and its association with Stanlow traffic was reinforced by having each locomotive named after a species of shell. A small number of Class 37s were brought into the pool from November 1989 onwards; the 37s were useful for working singly over lines with a low route availability, such as the Cambrian main line to Aberystwyth, and were also used to assist Class 47s with 1,400-tonne loads on the first part of their journey to Leeds and Jarrow.

A number of smaller distribution terminals served from Stanlow lost their rail service in the late 1980s and early 1990s, including Maxwelltown, Ulverston, Harrogate, York Foss Islands, Scarborough, Doe Hill, Warsop, Torksey, Aberystwyth, Swindon, Newbury and Peterborough, together with the liquid petroleum gas depot at Rowley Regis. But the heaviest flows held up well during this period, with nine booked trains each week to Leeds and seven to Jarrow. BR Trainload Freight signed a long-term contract with Shell in late 1992 that resulted in a further increase to 12 trains a week to Jarrow. The use of Class 60s on Stanlow traffic was delayed because the siding layout at the refinery prevented the operation of suitably long trains for Class 60 haulage; however, the Leeds and Jarrow services went over to Class 60 haulage in 1993.

The optimism created by the Jarrow contract

Petroleum-liveried No 37418 *Pectinidae* passes the loading racks at Stanlow with fuel oil for Pilkington's at Cowley Hill on 8 July 1991.

The last revenue-earning freight on Cambrian lines was oil to Aberystwyth, which lasted until April 1993. Nos 20170 and 20040 run round their train in Aberystwyth station on 5 April 1988 after working 6J28, the 0100 departure from Stanlow.

Above Some infrequent petroleum trains did not appear in the working timetable. The flow from Stanlow to Scarborough operated about once a month by special arrangement. No 37430 *Cwmbran* passes Kirkham Abbey with 7Z59, the 1610 Scarborough to Stanlow empties, on 16 July 1990.

Below No 37718 sets out from Runcorn Folly Lane with 6P32, the 13.45 empties to Stanlow, on 23 April 1993. A curiosity of this working was that the loaded train took the one-way chord between Frodsham and Halton Junction while the return train had a much longer route involving reversals at Hartford and Warrington.

flows adding up to barely one train a day, the cost of keeping the rail loading facility at Stanlow operational could no longer be justified, and it was therefore no surprise when the last loaded tank train left in March 1998.

Bitumen from Ellesmere Port was conveyed in a mixture of trainload and wagonload consignments in BR days. Trainload services operated from Ellesmere Port to Skipton and Bardon Hill and wagonload destinations included Culloden Moor, Elswick, Hereford and Norwich. However, the remaining flows ceased in early 1990 when Shell moved its bitumen production to another, non-rail-connected, site.

•

The BP refinery at Grangemouth began operations in 1921. A massive expansion programme was completed in the early 1970s, which brought the refining capacity up to 8.6 million tonnes per year. The railway benefited from this expansion, establishing a network of receiving terminals throughout Scotland. Much of the traffic was conveyed by the wagonload, but trainload services operated in the 1980s to distribution terminals ranging from Bishopbriggs – a mere hop of 25 miles from Grangemouth – to Jarrow and Dalston over the English border.

The Bishopbriggs flow was an obvious target for closure as many of its customers could easily be served from Grangemouth directly by road; its closure in May 1994 caused a 30% reduction in the rail-borne output from Grangemouth refinery. Other losses in the early 1990s were individually smaller but cumulatively significant, as BR Trainload Freight was forced to provide its own resources for flows that had previously moved by Speedlink. Those losses included traffic to Aberdeen, Inverness, Perth, Leuchars, Mallaig, Corpach, Fort William, Oban, Connel Ferry, Wishaw, Paisley, Maxwelltown and virtually all ScotRail fuelling points. All that remained after 1994 was a daily train from Grangemouth to Dalston, together with a weekly path to each of Prestwick, Riccarton, Linkswood and Motherwell.

A turnaround in rail traffic from Grangemouth was heralded in December 2000 when BP received a £10 million grant for new loading facilities at the refinery and several new or refurbished receiving

The Maxwelltown branch survived for petroleum deliveries long after it stopped handling general freight traffic. No 08396 awaits permission to proceed with empty tanks from Maxwelltown to Dumfries yard on 24 August 1981.

failed to stem the gradual decline of rail-borne traffic from Stanlow. A major blow was the closure of the Shell distribution terminal at Leeds in 1995, causing the loss of a daily 1,000-tonne trainload. By the end of 1996 the only substantial flow from Stanlow was the twice-daily service to Jarrow. However, it was then decided that Jarrow would receive all its supplies from Immingham instead of Stanlow from early 1998. The only remaining rail business from Stanlow would then be intermittent trainloads to the distribution terminal at Whittington, to industrial users at Oakleigh, Lostock, Cowley Hill and Ravenhead, and occasional gas oil traffic to Chester. With these

Stanlow and Ellesmere Port petroleum train plan, October 1970

Code	Dep	Days	From	To
6D39	0350	WFO - Q	Stanlow	Colwick
6K39	0350	TThSO	Stanlow	Cliffe Vale
6K39	0350	WFO - Q	Stanlow	Uttoxeter
6P39	0352	WFO - Q	Ellesmere Port	Derby
6J30	0416	MSX - Q	Stanlow	Whittington
6J30	0416	MX - Q	Stanlow	Marchwiel
6J30	0416	MX - Q	Stanlow	Shrewsbury Coton Hill
6P34	0438	MSX - Q	Stanlow	Heysham
6F42	0438	MSX - Q	Stanlow	Ravenhead
6D33	0628	SO	Stanlow	Toton
6F37	0826	SX	Stanlow	Oakleigh or Sandbach
6G36	1100	SX - Q	Stanlow	Washwood Heath
6E52	1245	SX	Stanlow	Ecclesfield
6F43	1433	SX	Stanlow	Haydock
6M31	1944	SX	Stanlow	Doe Hill
6G37	1920	SX	Ellesmere Port	Bedworth
6E37	2048	SX	Ellesmere Port	Gainsborough, Tuxford or Warsop
6O40	2007	SX - Q	Ellesmere Port	Wareham
6F34	2156	MThO	Ellesmere Port	Bardon Hill
6H34	2156	TWFO	Ellesmere Port	Rowley Regis
6G34	2152	TWFO	Stanlow	Longbridge

Stanlow and Ellesmere Port petroleum sample programme, August 1989

Code	Dep	Days	From	To
6P41	0021	TFSO	Stanlow	Dalston
6E15	0047	WFSO	Stanlow	Jarrow
6Z34	0055	WO	Stanlow	Newbury
6Z33	0055	FO	Stanlow	Oxford
6J28	0116	WO	Stanlow	Aberystwyth
6Z98	0135	WO	Stanlow	York
6E37	0230	SX	Stanlow	Leeds
6Z74	0300	WO	Stanlow	Hereford
6J26	0306	TFO	Stanlow	Whittington
6P37	0357	TThO	Ellesmere Port	Skipton
6P43	0420	ThO	Stanlow	Preston Docks
6Z35	0436	FO	Stanlow	Peterborough
6Z35	0436	WO	Stanlow	Barnwell Jn
6R72	0510	ThO	Stanlow	Ulverston
6R37	0550	WFO	Stanlow	Oakleigh
6F53	0614	TO	Stanlow	Ravenhead
6E25	0637	MSX	Stanlow	Leeds
6E18	0756	FSX	Stanlow	Jarrow
6G43	1329	MO	Stanlow	West Bromwich
6F34	2130	ThO	Ellesmere Port	Bardon Hill

Grangemouth petroleum sample programme, August 1992				
Code	**Dep**	**Days**	**From**	**To**
6H33	0145	MSX	Grangemouth	Inverness
7Y43	0340	ThO	Grangemouth	Connel Ferry
6D35	0400	WThSO	Grangemouth	Hawkhead
7Y45	0442	TO	Grangemouth	Oban
6L11	0516	MO	Grangemouth	Perth
6L49	0516	FO	Grangemouth	St Fort
6D27	0640	TO	Grangemouth	Wishaw
6N04	0725	MO	Grangemouth	Corkerhill, Motherwell, Eastfield
6N04	0800	SO	Grangemouth	Edinburgh
6D39	1050	MX	Grangemouth	Mossend
6N70	1410	TWFO	Grangemouth	Bishopbriggs
6N04	1535	MWO	Grangemouth	Bowling
6E58	1956	WO	Grangemouth	Jarrow
7Y33	2015	FSX	Grangemouth	Fort William
6M34	2350	MSX	Grangemouth	Dalston

Left The West Highland line carried several petroleum flows until the early 1990s. No 37410 is pictured at Oban on 15 July 1992 before working the 1649 departure to Grangemouth.

Right No 20119 heads a train of empty bitumen tanks down the rarely used Ardrossan Harbour branch on 18 July 1984. After loading, the tanks will form an evening departure to Culloden Moor.

terminals. The announcement promised the return of petroleum traffic to Fort William, Lairg, Kilmarnock, Maxwelltown and Aberdeen. The flows to Fort William and Lairg started in 2001, using EWS Enterprise services, but at the time of writing there has still been no sign of a revival at the other three locations. The Lairg traffic became the only freight flow on the Highland main line, therefore effectively operating as a very short block train.

In addition to traffic from Grangemouth, BR carried bitumen from Ardrossan Harbour to Culloden Moor until 1984 and wagonloads of fuel oil from the Esso storage depot at Bowling to Oban and Mallaig throughout the 1980s. The Mallaig traffic was conveyed on the back of a passenger train between Fort William and Mallaig until Sprinter units took over in 1989 – the last example of mixed passenger/freight working on the BR network.

Gas oil

Until the 1980s gas oil – fuel for diesel locomotives and units – was conveyed to BR motive power depots and fuelling points by means of general wagonload services. Very few depots were busy enough to justify regular deliveries by block train, and in any case most had track layouts that could only take a few wagons at a time. But the withdrawal of Speedlink in July 1991 forced BR to find new arrangements for distributing gas oil.

Either the traffic would have to be transferred to road, or a dedicated train plan would have to be devised in order to connect five refineries with well over 50 depots and fuelling points.

BR's Trainload Freight management opted to keep as much gas oil traffic on rail as possible. A few depots such as Selhurst and Ripple Lane switched to taking oil by road, but the majority of depots continued to receive their fuel by rail from one of five designated refineries – Fawley, Shell Haven, Lindsey, Stanlow and Grangemouth – as listed in the table on page 125.

Fawley supplied most of its depots using a network of Trainload Petroleum-sponsored services, some of which had already been introduced in 1989 when it was clear that Speedlink was being run down. The West Midlands depots had received their oil from a pipeline terminal at Bromford Bridge until 1990 but were now served by rail from Fawley, using the same train that carried bitumen to Bromford Bridge and LPG to Longport.

Gas oil from Shell Haven started its journey on one of two weekly trains: one ran to Harwich with traffic for Colchester, Ipswich and Norwich, and the other ran to Temple Mills and Ferme Park. Temple Mills was the detaching point for flows to Cambridge and to Southern Region destinations, which would use a combination of scheduled RfD services, CivilLink engineers' trains and spare locomotive movements to complete their journeys.

Lindsey refinery continued to supply all fuelling

Gas oil for the diesel multiple unit depot at Marylebone was conveyed by an occasional trip working from Willesden Yard, with reversals at Acton Canal Wharf and Neasden Junction. No 25301 has just completed its run-round movement at Neasden Junction with the loaded tanks on 6 April 1983.

points in the northern half of the former Eastern Region. In January 1993 Trainload Petroleum operated four trains a week for gas oil from Lindsey: one bound for Tinsley, and three to Healey Mills. The Healey Mills train called at Knottingley depot in the outward direction and fed into the CivilLink network at Healey Mills Yard.

Stanlow once supplied gas oil to depots as far north as Ayr and as far east as March, Cambridge and Norwich. After 1991 its lost these destinations but still served much of the East Midlands as well as North West England and North Wales. In January 1993 most of the gas oil from Stanlow to North West depots was covered by one locomotive diagram, serving different locations on different days. The arrangements for serving Buxton were particularly intricate: tanks were conveyed by the Stanlow to Allerton train as far as Ditton, where they joined a trainload of cement empties from Ditton to Peak Forest; they then travelled to Buxton by what would otherwise be a light engine movement to the depot. Itineraries such as this were an operational headache and led to very poor wagon productivity, but Buxton depot was an awkward location to

A single gas oil tank for Lincoln fuelling point is propelled across the main line at Pelham Street by pilot loco No 08242 on 26 July 1984.

PETROLEUM

BR gas oil traffic, January 1993

Refinery:	Fawley	Shell Haven	Lindsey	Stanlow	Grangemouth
Fuelling points:	Eastleigh	Dover	Cleethorpes	Chester	Craigentinny
	Bournemouth	Ashford	Immingham	Holyhead	Millerhill
	Fratton	Willesden	Frodingham	Allerton	Motherwell
	Penzance	Bletchley	Doncaster	Buxton	Ayr
	St Blazey	Ferme Park	Neville Hill	Longsight	Perth
	Laira	Cambridge	Holbeck	Newton Heath	Aberdeen
	Bristol	March	Tinsley	Springs Branch	Inverness
	Margam	Colchester	Knottingley	Carlisle	
	Cardiff Canton	Ipswich	Thornaby	Crewe	
	Old Oak Common	Norwich	Heaton	Leicester	
	Reading		Shirebrook	Toton	
	Bescot			Derby	
	Saltley				
	Tyseley				
	Soho				

serve by road. Gas oil from Stanlow to Holyhead was conveyed as far as Llandudno Junction by the daily chemicals train from Ellesmere Port to Amlwch; the locomotive from that train then made an out-and-back trip from Llandudno Junction to Holyhead during its layover time, carrying vans for Anglesey Aluminium as well as the gas oil. The East Midlands depots were served by a dedicated 'round robin' train calling at Crewe, Leicester, Toton and Derby, an apparently simpler journey than those to Holyhead or Buxton but one that took 16 hours to complete.

The transfer of Scottish gas oil traffic from Speedlink to dedicated trains began in November 1989 when Petroleum sub-sector trip workings were introduced from Grangemouth to fuelling points in the Glasgow and Edinburgh areas. By January 1993 various solutions had been found for other Scottish depots. Gas oil traffic for Ayr used the Glasgow area trip as far as Mossend yard and

After the demise of Speedlink, several fuelling points continued to receive gas oil by rail using complex sequences of train services. No 90146 passes Caledonian Road in North London with a Railfreight Distribution service from Ipswich to Wembley on 15 June 1995, conveying empty tanks for Fawley. The tanks will continue their journey on a Connectrail service from Wembley to Washwood Heath, where they will join a petroleum service from Longport to Fawley.

The First Great Western depot at Long Rock, Penzance, continued to receive its gas oil by rail in the 21st century, with a weekly trip working from St Blazey or Burngullow. No 66160 awaits its path on to the main line at Penzance with 6C11, the 1230 empties to St Blazey, on 18 April 2006.

was then attached to a Trainload Coal service to Falkland Yard, Ayr. Fuel for Inverness was conveyed via Millerhill and used the Trainload Freight 'bulklink' service between Millerhill and Inverness, a service that had been introduced in 1989 to carry cement, liquid petroleum gas and coal as well as BR gas oil. Fuel for Perth and Aberdeen was conveyed by a Railfreight Distribution service between Mossend and Aberdeen, another very mixed train that also carried cement from Oxwellmains, china clay from Cornwall and paper from Aberdeen to mainland Europe.

After 1993 the number of gas oil flows diminished sharply as some depots closed and others adopted road deliveries. All flows from Shell Haven ceased in 1993 when the refinery closed its rail loading facility. In some cases gas oil was left to pick up a larger share of costs because of the loss of other freight flows. An example of this

was Holyhead, which had to be served by a dedicated train from Stanlow after the chemical traffic to and from Amlwch finished and switched to road deliveries in May 1996. However, some of the surviving gas oil flows were accommodated on the Enterprise network launched by Transrail in 1994 and later developed by EWS.

By late 2007 little remained of the once comprehensive network of gas oil trains, with just two refineries forwarding gas oil. Lindsey supplied Doncaster, Neville Hill, Thornaby and Bescot, mostly using scheduled Enterprise trains but with a dedicated weekly feeder service from Doncaster to Neville Hill. Fawley supplied Eastleigh, Ipswich, Margam, Bristol St Philips Marsh, Laira and Penzance. The Ipswich and Margam traffic was conveyed by scheduled Enterprise services via Wembley, with the Ipswich tanks travelling between Wembley and Harwich on an intermodal train. Bristol was served by a direct weekly train from Fawley, while Laira and Penzance traffic shared haulage with the twice-weekly bitumen tanks from Fawley to Plymouth Cattewater. All flows used two-axle TTA/TUA tanks except for Neville Hill, which received some of its oil in bogie TEA tanks.

Index